Praise for
The Flow of Time and Money

"*The Flow of Time and Money* is the ideal introduction for those seeking to create lasting wealth and enjoy their lives."
 — Dr. Carver Mead,
   Caltech Professor and Silicon Valley Pioneer

"Dr. Watts has taken the secrets of wealth creation and personal productivity and made them accessible to everyone. With ever longer lifespans becoming a reality, this is a must read for achieving financial security!"
 — Ray Kurzweil,
   author of *The Singularity is Near* and
   Fantastic Voyage: Live Long Enough to Live Forever

"Author Lloyd Watts has written a book that could not be more timely given the woes that spell out the US economy right now... *The Flow of Time and Money* is a blueprint with a refreshing formula that makes every bit of sense how to grow your bank account in these hard times."
 — Michael Dresser,
   The Michael Dresser Show, Lifestyle Talk Radio Network

"*The Flow of Time and Money* by Lloyd Watts is a book everyone should pick up and read if they are concerned about their own personal economic health as we go into a new year with a new President."
 — Jon Duvall, *National Public Radio*

"Inspired... If we, as teenagers, got the kind of financial education *The Flow of Time and Money* provides, we would not be in such dire economic straits today."
 — John Lehman, *Bookreview.com*

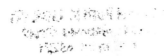

The Flow of Time and Money

How to Create a Full and Prosperous Life

Lloyd Watts, PhD

Published by
Megawatt Media Corporation
1931 Old Middlefield Way, Suite 221
Mountain View, CA 94043

This material is for general informational purposes only. Readers
should use their own judgment or consult a financial planner before
making specific investment decisions.

Designed by Megawatt Media.
Printed in the United States of America

Watts, D. Lloyd
The Flow of Time and Money: How to Create a Full and Prosperous
Life / Lloyd Watts

ISBN: 0980153719
EAN-13: 9780980153712

Contents

For my lovely daughters
Stephanie and Michelle

Introduction

This book is the condensation of 32 years of study and experiment in how to live life to the fullest. Every time I have learned or developed a new technique for making my life more effective, I have put it to work, and kept it only if it actually made a difference and fit in with the other approaches that I have adopted.

I believe that how we spend our time and our money determines our fate. If you waste your time and waste your money, your life will be unfulfilling and impoverished. Invest your time in your education, relationships, health, and skills, and invest your money in assets that provide for you and your loved ones, and your life will be fulfilling and full of comforts and pleasures, with a legacy worth leaving behind. Only you can decide how you will spend your time and your money, and what you will make of your life.

Unfortunately, the principles of time and money are not taught in schools, and most people are launched into adulthood without a clear understanding of how to live their lives to their full potential. The 2008 economic meltdown is a spectacular example of what can go wrong when individuals, corporations, and even nations steer away from the fundamental teachings in this book.

In *The Flow of Time and Money*, I make the principles of time and money simple, by using pictures to show how time and money flow and accumulate in their various forms. I sincerely hope that these insights will be of service to you. May you live your life to the fullest!

Acknowledgments

I would like to acknowledge those friends who contributed to the book, or otherwise helped in its creation. In particular, I would like to thank:

—Valery Lloyd-Watts, my mother, for her constant, loving support, and for her steady supply of inspirational reading, which helped to create the framework for this book.

—Donald Watts, my father, for his inspiration and support throughout my life.

—Allan Crawford, my Canadian mentor, for inspiring me to enter the world of business, and for his support of my education and early investment in my first business.

—Carver Mead, my Caltech professor, for his wisdom and support, both as my professor and as an investor and board member in my first business.

—Paul Allen, whose long-term support has made it possible for my first business to survive and prosper.

—Peter Santos and the rest of the team at Audience, who have turned an exciting technology vision into a thriving business.

—Tsung-I Ho, who translated the book into Chinese and helped introduce the book to new friends in a new part of the world.

—Laura Brisbee, who introduced me to photography and took the author photograph at the back of the book.

—Stephanie Watts, who took the photograph that adorns the front cover of the book.

—Denise Garcia, who has provided much-appreciated encouragement and assistance during the preparations for the launch of the book.

—Ludovico Capuzzo, who has enthusiastically catalyzed a substantial effort to bring this message to a much larger international audience.

—Henry McGilton, whose insights and keen eye for aesthetics have helped to make the book concise and beautiful.

—Silke Lindner, Jeff Barboni, and Onur Tackin, who, along with Ludovico and Henry, are helping to shape a new educational foundation.

—Charlie Barrett, Alan Waldman, and the team at the Barrett Company in Los Angeles, who have brought their considerable talents to help promote this book.

—Amy Collins at The Cadence Group, and Gwyn Snider, who created the beautiful new cover design and are now leading the sales and distribution efforts.

Lloyd Watts, Mountain View, California
November 1, 2008.

Part I

Money, Time, Life and Wealth

Money, Time, Life and Wealth

If you want to have a full and prosperous life, you need to understand how time and money work. Some principles are unfailingly true, yet are not obvious to all of us without some form of teaching. I have been fortunate to have some gifted and generous teachers, and I have sought out knowledge of how time and money work from every source I could find. I offer to pass my knowledge on to you.

Time and Money are fundamentally linked, as I will show in pictures soon. I will start with how money works, and then show how the principles that govern the Flow of Money are really the same as the principles that govern the Flow of Time. Let us begin with a look at how money flows.

The Flow of Money

Most of us have a job and pay taxes. We have expenses and we buy things. And most of us vaguely wish we could get a raise so we could save more and maybe become wealthy some day.

If that's the plan, it's not going to happen. We may get the raise, but we won't become wealthy without a much better understanding of how the money is flowing through our lives and the social forces acting upon us. To make it easier to see the elements in our financial lives, I am going to use pictures, and a familiar analogy for something that flows, namely, water in a leaky bucket.

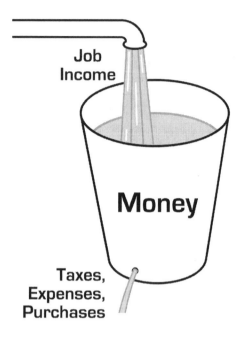

For most people in the middle class, their financial lives are like a leaky bucket. They have job income, which is poured into their bucket by their employer, and the money leaks out in the form of expenses, purchases and taxes. All they have to show for their financial lives is the possessions they've bought over the years—cars, furniture, TVs, etc. Usually, these possessions are worth a lot less than they originally cost.

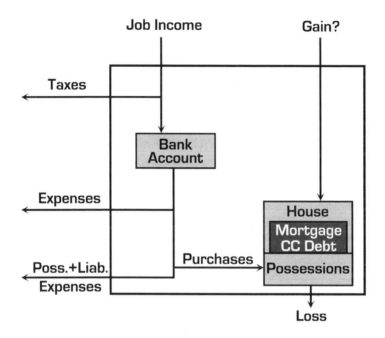

The Flow of Money for the Middle Class

Here, I am showing this same idea but in more detail. **The job income** is flowing in the top, and **taxes** are being taken out before the money gets to your **bank account**. Then the money flows out to pay **expenses** (food, clothing, vacations, etc.) What's left is usually used to **purchase possessions** like furniture, cars, TVs, etc. Unfortunately, the value of those possessions goes down after you buy them, so I am showing the **loss** of value as another leak out of the bucket. But, here's the part that most people don't realize: *Some possessions actually trigger more expenses.* For example, a car costs you money not just when you buy it, but also every time you put gas and oil in it, when you repair it, buy tires for it, buy insurance for it, license it, smog-check it, etc. You wouldn't have any of those expenses if you didn't own the car. So, I call those expenses

triggered expenses, since they are triggered by owning the possession. Similarly, if you have credit card debt, you have to make payments and pay service charges on those debts—that's a Liability-Triggered Expense. Finally, what about your house? If you own a house with a mortgage, you have your monthly mortgage payment, so that's another kind of Liability-triggered expense. But the house itself triggers expenses, too—for example, house insurance, property taxes, utility bills, higher needs for furniture, maintenance costs, etc. Technically, the house is an asset, but it has the nasty property of triggering expenses.

So, here is the first reason why the middle class struggles so much. As their income goes up, they buy nicer cars and houses, which trigger higher expenses, thus ensuring that their expenses always rise to the level of their new income. In the leaky bucket analogy, getting a raise is like opening up the faucet—so we poke bigger holes in the bucket to make sure the bucket stays empty!

So, how do we break the cycle of rising income and rising expenses? Do what the Rich do: Invest in assets that will trigger passive income and capital gains.

Here's the general picture of personal finance:

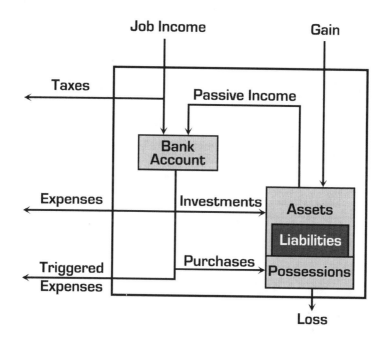

The Flow of Money (general case)

The new element in the picture is that we can now make **investments** in **assets**, and those assets may trigger both **passive income** (money that comes in because you own the asset), and **capital gains** (increase in value while you hold the asset).

Many people don't really know what kinds of investments will create passive income. Some examples of assets and their corresponding passive income include:

ASSET	PASSIVE INCOME
Stocks	Dividends
Bonds	Yield
Promissory Notes	Interest
Real Estate	Rents
Intellectual Property	Royalties, License Fees
Businesses	Business Cash Flow

Assets and the kind of Passive Income they produce

If you want to be wealthy, you will want to buy or create this kind of asset, the kind that produces positive cash flow for you. This is money you can live on while your assets work for you.

Note that your house is technically an asset from an accounting point of view, but it does not produce passive income for you—it actually triggers BIG expenses. So this is the next secret of the rich: **The Rich buy and create assets that produce Passive Income and Capital Gains.** The middle class incurs debt and buys possessions that produce Triggered Expenses and Capital Losses. If you want to become wealthy, live in a modest home, so you will keep your expenses down and have money left over to invest in Income-Producing Assets.

If you are going to put money aside to buy assets, you will need a place to put that money where it won't be confused with money you want for living expenses. I recommend creating a new account for your investing fund, at a different institution than your bank. If you keep your investing fund at your bank, you will be tempted to make transfers from your investing fund to your chequing account. Overdraft protection is an example of a careless way you may accidentally deplete your investing fund. That money is for investing, not spending! Put it in a different place. I use a Schwab account to hold my investing fund.

 If you follow the above advice and create a special account for your investing fund, your leaky bucket will now have a special "cup" in it, from which the money won't be able to leak out to the expenses. This is how the rich got started—transferring money from their job income into their investing fund, thus accumulating capital they could use to buy assets. In this phase, they are developing the habit of **Paying Themselves First**—make sure money goes into the investing fund before it goes out in expenses.

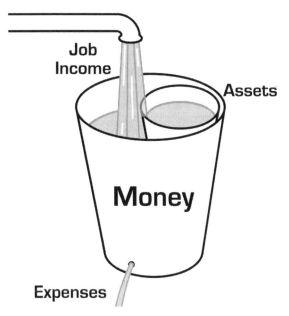

Eventually, the assets begin to create Passive Income, thus reducing your dependence on Job Income.

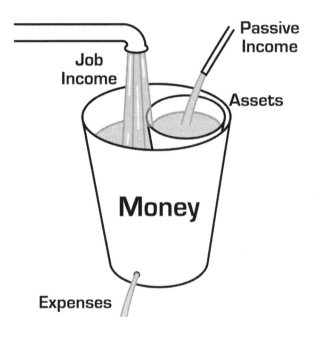

Finally, the Assets have grown large enough to produce a large Passive Income, and the Job Income is no longer needed at all. When your Passive Income can cover your Expenses, you have reached Financial Independence. You don't have to work for money any more. Your money works for you!

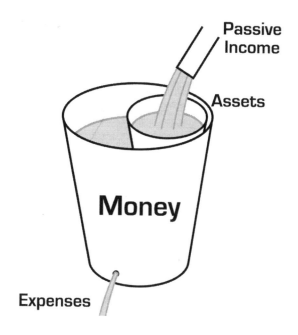

Here is the detailed version of the figure, showing the Flow of Money for the Rich or Financially Independent.

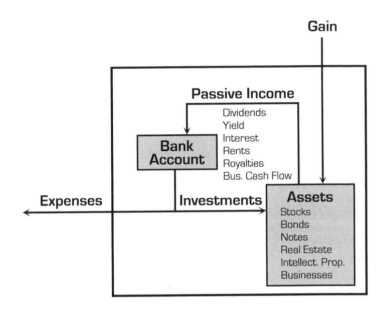

The Flow of Money for the Rich

In this figure, there is no job income, just passive income from your assets. This passive income is able to pay for your expenses, so job income is not required. As long as the expenses are kept at this level, you could sustain this life indefinitely. You don't work for money any more—your money is now working for you!

So, in principle, that is how to transition from Middle Class to Financially Independent. Pay Yourself First, Accumulate

Capital, Buy Assets that produce Passive Income, until that Passive Income equals your expenses. Sounds easy, right? Until you try to do it. That's when you find out that changing your flow of money requires effort, self-education, and consistent daily action toward long-term goals. All of these relate to how you manage your time. So, now we need to look at the Flow of Time.

The Flow of Time

Here's the good news. The Flow of Time is almost identical to the Flow of Money—if you're with me so far, the next part is going to look very familiar! I have deliberately kept the discussion parallel so you will be able to see that there is a very close correspondence between the Flow of Time and the Flow of Money.

We all get 168 hours each week to work with. Most of us put in 40 hours each week at a job. We spend time sleeping, eating, bathing, shopping, commuting, having a beer, watching the game. And most of us vaguely wish we had more time so we could make more of our lives.

If that's the plan, it's not going to happen. If we want to lead a full and rewarding life, we need a much better understanding of how the time is flowing through our lives and the social forces acting upon us.

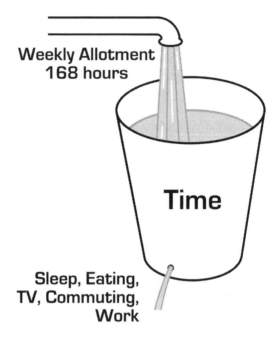

For most people, their use of time is like a leaky bucket. They get their weekly allotment of 168 hours, and the time leaks out in the form of sleeping, eating, working, commuting, watching TV, etc. What do we have to show for the time we've been given? Didn't we dream once of doing something great with our lives?

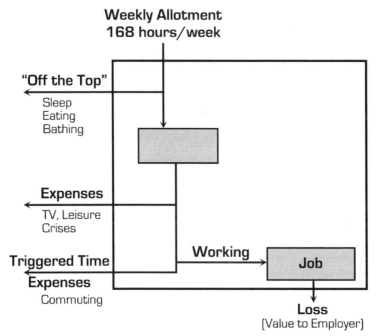

The Flow of Time for the average person

In the next figure, I am showing this same idea but in more detail. Our **weekly allotment of 168 hours/week** is flowing in the top, and the **off-the-top expenses** (sleep, eating, bathing) are being taken out before we even have a choice about how to spend our time. Then the time flows out to our discretionary **expenses** (leisure time, watching TV, handling crises, etc.) The other major use of our time is **working** at our **job**. Unfortunately, the value of your work time goes to your employer, who makes money on your work, so I am showing this work time as a **loss** to you. But, don't forget, you are giving your employer this time in exchange for your job income, so you are getting something out of it. But, here's the part that most people don't realize: *Some activities actually trigger more expenses of your time.* For example, not only do you spend time at your job, but you also have to commute to your job, travel occasionally, buy clothes for work, etc. You wouldn't have to spend any of that time if you didn't have the job. So, I call those time expenses **triggered time expenses**, since they are triggered by the primary activity you are doing. Other activities trigger time expenses too. For example, you may decide to take up skiing. This enjoyable leisure activity will trigger other time expenses, such as driving to your favorite mountain, shopping for equipment and clothes, lessons, etc.

So, here is the second reason why the middle class struggles so much. As their careers advance, they take up more and more time-consuming activities, which trigger new expenses of their time. In the leaky bucket analogy, getting another week of vacation time is like opening up the faucet (we have more time to work with)—so we poke bigger holes in the bucket to make sure the bucket stays empty!

So, how do we get more time to accomplish our life's dreams? Do what the Fulfilled do: Invest your time in life assets that enable to you to accomplish more in less time, and to help other people. Here's the general picture of personal time management:

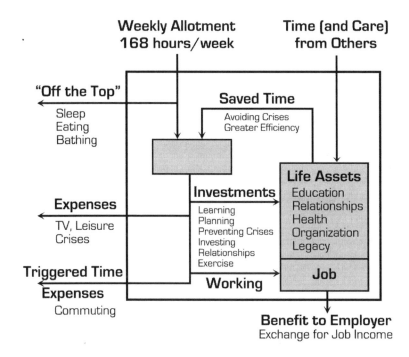

The Flow of Time (general case)

The new element in the picture is that we can now make **investments** in **life assets**, and those assets may result in **saved time and increased effectiveness** (so you have more time to do other things), and **time and care from others** (who help you because they see you will be able to help them).

Many people don't really know what kinds of life assets will create saved time and increased effectiveness. Some examples of life assets and their corresponding passive income include:

LIFE ASSET	SAVED TIME
Education	Accomplish more in less time.
Relationships	Less time arguing, more cooperation
Health	Less sick time
Organization	Less duplication of effort, fewer crises

Life Assets and the ways they save time and increase effectiveness

If you want to be fulfilled, you will want to invest your time in this kind of life asset, the kind that produces saved time and increased effectiveness for you and the people you care about.

So this is the next secret of the Fulfilled: **The Fulfilled invest their time in Life Assets that increase their effectiveness and save them time.** The average person wastes time on activities that dull the senses and don't increase effectiveness in any way. If you want to become fulfilled, waste as little time as possible on life-depleting activities, and invest your time in your education, relationships, health and organization.

If you follow the above advice and begin to invest your time in your education, health, relationships and organization, your leaky bucket will now have a special "cup" in it. This cup represents your Life Assets. One of the principles of fulfillment is to invest first in these life assets before spending time on other discretionary activities.   In time as well as money, **Pay Yourself First.**

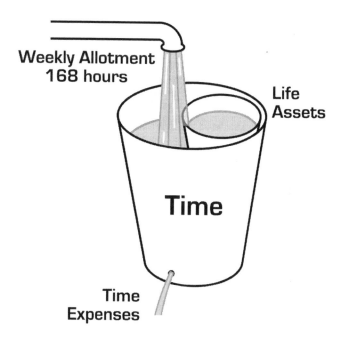

Weekly Allotment 168 hours

Life Assets

Time

Time Expenses

Eventually, these life assets begin to save you time and increase your effectiveness, partly through the received Time (and Care) from others. For example, any time a friend or mentor teaches you something, they are contributing to your life assets.

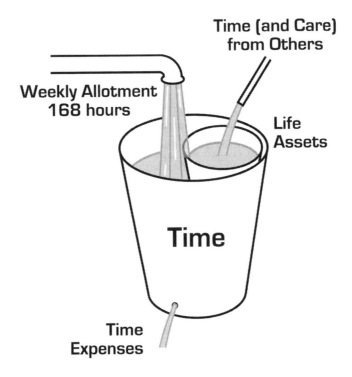

When you are successful, personally and financially, you will no longer need to work for someone else. Your life assets will include your sound financial education and experience, which will enable you to create material assets whose Passive Income will pay your expenses. This is the Flow of Time for the Fulfilled and Financially Independent:

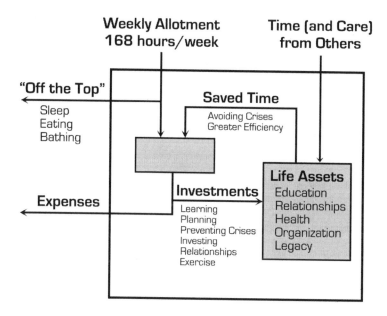

The Flow of Time for the Fulfilled and Financially Independent

In this figure, no time is spent working for someone else, nor is any time spent commuting to a job. The life assets of your education, relationships, health and organization allow you to create material assets that provide your passive income.

So, in principle, that is how to transition from unfulfilled to fulfilled. Invest your time in your education, relationships, health and organization, thus increasing your life assets, and your ability to provide for yourself materially, provide for your loved ones, and make a difference to the world.

So, we have seen that the structure of Time and the structure of Money have the same form and flow characteristics. Now, the next step is to show how they couple together.

The Flow of Life

It's no coincidence that Time and Money have the same structural form. They are really different forms of the same underlying thing. Some people call it Life Energy, or Life, or Chi—there are lots of different names for it and ways of looking at it and talking about it. But, if they are really the same thing, how does one get converted into the other?

The poor and middle class do it the easy way. They spend their time working for money, and their employer does the conversion for them. On the next page, I show how the systems couple together for the poor and middle class. We get our 168 hours/week, which is spent sleeping, eating, bathing, watching TV, commuting and working. Our employer pays us for that work, and we spend the money on taxes, food, shelter, entertainment, and toys. At the end of a life, what do we have to show for it? We gave our life energy to our employer, and we have a pile of toys that are worth a lot less than what we paid for them.

This bleak picture is obviously an oversimplification, to highlight the main features of working for someone else. This way of life is what some people call the Treadmill or the Rat Race, and generally leads to a feeling that "there must be more to life than this."

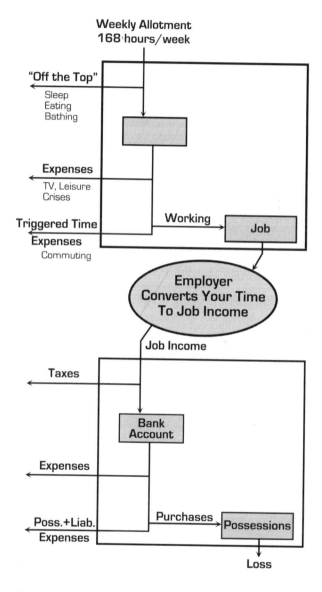

Weekly Allotment
168 hours/week

"Off the Top"
  Sleep
  Eating
  Bathing

Expenses
  TV, Leisure
  Crises

Triggered Time
Expenses
  Commuting

Working

Job

Employer
Converts Your Time
To Job Income

Job Income

Taxes

Bank
Account

Expenses

Poss.+Liab.
Expenses

Purchases

Possessions

Loss

The Flow of Life for the Poor and Middle Class

We can get out of this Treadmill way of life by beginning to invest our time in our Life Assets, and by investing our money into material assets that create passive income and capital gains. If we do, the picture looks like this:

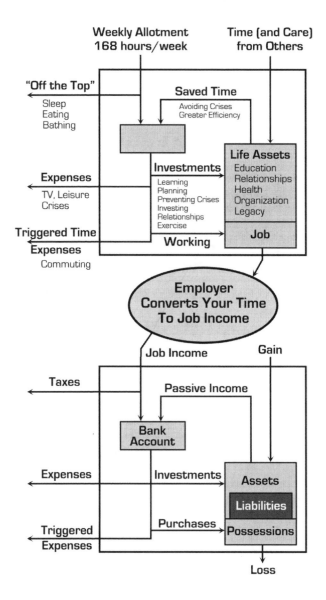

The Flow of Life (general case)

And finally, when you have increased your financial education to the point where your material assets provide enough passive income for you to live on, you won't need an employer, and your flow of life will look like this:

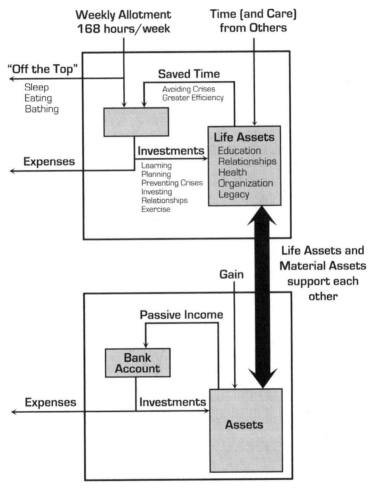

**The Flow of Life for the Fulfilled and
Financially Independent**

So now, the two systems do not need an employer to join your time and your money together. You have assumed complete responsibility for your own life and success. A new linkage is formed between your Life Assets and your Material Assets, and **you** are the one gloriously making it happen. Your life assets are responsible for creating and maintaining your material assets. And your material assets provide for your living expenses, so you don't have to work for someone else, thus giving you more time to grow your life assets.

Here is my shorthand for this interaction:

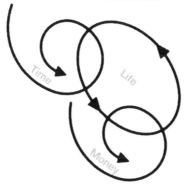

The swirl in the upper left represents the investment of time into your life assets. The swirl in the lower right represents the investment of money into your material assets. And the loop in the upper right is the interaction that occurs when your material assets and your life assets support and build each other. I believe that this is where wealth and personal strength are to be found. And this is the springboard for making your contribution to the world, which I will discuss in the last chapter of this book.

If you want to be wealthy and fulfilled, don't waste your time and money—focus on your Life Assets and your Material Assets!

Wealth and Survival Time

We all talk about wealth as though we understand what it is, but how many of us have really sat down and thought about it? My dictionary defines it as "abundance of valuable material possessions or resources." Is that it? Is it just how much stuff you have? Your net worth?

Buckminster Fuller sat down and thought about it. I mean, he *really* thought about it. In *Approaching the Benign Environment,* he said,

> "… what we probably mean by 'wealth', really, has something to do with how many forward days we have arranged for our environment to take care of us and regenerate us in life and give us increased degrees of freedom."

Fascinating. Fuller defines wealth not in terms of money but in terms of time—how many days into the future you can live on what you have—your **Survival Time**. It's your Net Worth, normalized by your net Expense rate. This beautiful definition spans cultures and currencies; it works even in bartering cultures where there is no concept of money—it even works for squirrels.   It could be how much food you have stored, divided by how fast you eat it.

So, let us try using this definition and see if it leads anywhere useful.   In terms of the leaky bucket analogy, your Survival Time is: how long it takes for your bucket to empty if you stop pouring into it from the top. How long could you live without your job, at your current lifestyle?

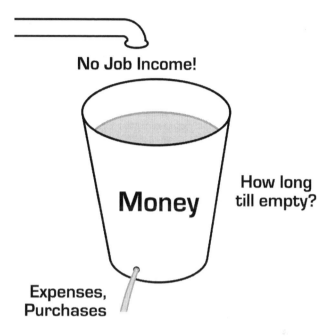

No Job Income!

Money

**How long
till empty?**

**Expenses,
Purchases**

Well, you can figure out how long it takes to drain the bucket if you know how much is in the bucket, and how fast it's leaking out. If you have $10,000 in the bucket, and you're spending $1,000 each month to stay alive, then you can live for 10 months, right?

For most people in the Middle Class, the amount in the bucket is what they have in their savings account, and their expenses are pretty much the same as their take-home pay (since they spend it all each month).

So, the formula for Survival Time for the Middle Class is

$$\text{Survival Time} = \frac{\text{Savings}}{\text{Expenses}}$$

Usually, people in the middle class arrange to have about two months of living expenses in their savings account. So, for example, they might have $6,000 in their savings account, but are spending $3,000 each month. If the savings get any larger than that, they quickly find a way to spend the excess.

Let's look at the situation for the financially independent. How long can they live if they lose their jobs? Well, they don't have a job in the first place, because their passive income is paying them. If their passive income is equal to their expenses, then the money is flowing *in* as fast as it flows *out*, so there is no net flow out of the bucket at all—that is, the bucket never empties because it is always being replenished by the passive income.

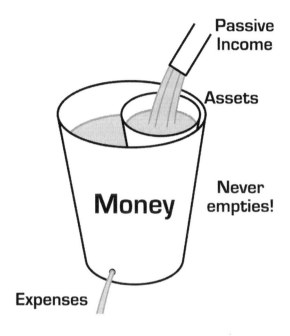

In this case, the formula for Survival Time for the Financially Independent is

$$\text{Survival Time} = \frac{\text{Net Worth}}{\text{Expenses} - \text{Passive Income}} = \text{Infinite}$$

In the general case, we ask, how long could we live at our current lifestyle without job income? That would mean, without selling our house, since we want to stay at our current lifestyle. That line of reasoning leads us to the general formula for Survival Time:

$$\text{Survival Time} = \frac{\text{Net Worth (not counting Home Equity)}}{\text{Expenses} - \text{Passive Income}}$$

That is, the amount in the bucket we can liquidate would be our net worth, but not counting our home equity, since we can't liquidate that if we are still living in the house. The net rate of flow out of the bucket is our Expenses, reduced by our Passive Income. Now, this formula tells us how to increase our Survival Time.

- Bigger Net Worth means longer survival time (you can live longer if you have more assets).
- Learn to invest beyond house, because your home equity doesn't help your Survival Time if you lose your job.
- Lower expenses means longer survival time (you can live longer if you spend at a lower rate).
- Bigger Passive Income means longer survival time (you can live longer if your assets pay you at a higher rate).

Why is this so important? Because it takes us out of the simple middle class view that "I could become wealthy if only I could get a raise." Job income doesn't even appear in the formula! No, the way to be wealthy is to invest in assets beyond your house, that increase your net worth and increase your passive income, while keeping your expenses low.

Note that I'm not discouraging anyone from buying a house. In fact, I think it's a good idea to own your own home.   I'm just recommending that you **keep your home expenses low**, and **learn to invest beyond your home**. When you've become financially independent, then you can reward yourself with a luxurious home.

Defining Wealth as Survival Time is an extremely useful and important idea, because it will guide you as you make financial decisions. Should I buy that expensive "status" car or the less expensive "transportation" car? The status car will decrease my net worth more, and give me higher maintenance costs, so it will lower my survival time more—ouch! The transportation car will also lower my survival time, but not nearly as much. Should I invest in that rental property across the street? Hmmm, it will increase my net worth and give me passive income, thus increasing my survival time—wow, how many of those can I get?

Once your passive income equals your expenses, your Survival Time becomes infinite, and we need a new meaning for Wealth. I would say that wealth creation goes through three stages:

1. **Survival Time.** In this stage, your Survival Time is finite and wealth creation is devoted to increasing passive income to equal expenses so as to make Survival Time infinite.
2. **Personal Financial Freedom.** In this stage, you have achieved the goal of making Survival Time infinite, but do not have sufficient excess passive income to be able to influence others. You may continue to increase your net worth and passive income, until you reach the stage of:
3. **Financial Influence.** In this stage, your passive income and net worth are large enough that you can begin to influence other people. This is the stage where philanthropy and contribution to the world can really begin.

Part II

Why We Struggle Financially

Why We Struggle Financially

We struggle financially because we fall into a number of traps. But why do we fall into the traps? For the same reason animals fall into a hunter's trap—because the traps are cleverly camouflaged, and there's tasty-looking bait in each one. They don't look like traps—they look like tempting food, so we go for it, and then discover later that it was trap. If you want to avoid falling into the traps, you need to know what the traps are, and why your instincts, education, and social pressures will tempt you into danger.

The Financial Traps

Accumulating Debt—"Borrow and Spend"

The first trap is the trap of accumulating consumer debt to buy possessions, such as cars, furnishings, TVs, stereos, etc. The tasty-looking bait is the possessions themselves, which are all shiny and new, and the admiration we get from our friends and family when we bring them home. The spiffy new widescreen TV, fabulous sports car, remodeled kitchen—they all inspire oohs and aahs from the people around us, and make us feel that all of our hard work over the years has finally been rewarded. *We've earned this*, we say to ourselves, as we hand over the credit card.

No, if you pay by using credit, you haven't earned it—you're going to have to pay for it handsomely over the months and years ahead. Credit card companies are routinely charging 19 percent interest on your consumer debt, and using every advertising trick they can to get you to buy more on credit.

I don't buy on credit. I have a debit card, which allows me to pay for things with the convenience of a card, but I don't ever use it to run up any kind of credit. If you do buy something with a credit card, do so only if you know you can pay it off as soon as the bill comes in.

This trap is a very hard one to get out of, for two reasons. Consumer borrowing is a very hard habit to break once you start, because you raise your lifestyle expectations well above your means without noticing it. Cutting back is painful. The other reason this trap is hard to escape is the high interest rates. Once you have a significant balance, you're now fighting that 19 percent interest rate, which is like swimming in a strong undertow in the ocean. The force gets stronger the deeper you go, and if you don't get out by a certain point, it can overwhelm you and lead directly to bankruptcy. Improper use of debt, at both the individual and corporate levels, was a major factor in the 2008 global economic meltdown.

If you have accumulated debt, you will see in the next chapter that your first step to financial health will be to pay it off. If you have not accumulated debt, congratulations — it will be important to maintain that good habit as you grow financially.

Regularly Depleting Savings—"Save and Spend"

The second trap is the trap of regularly depleting savings to purchase possessions. This trap prevents you from accumulating the necessary capital that will give you access to the interesting deals.

Here is the spending pattern of someone who practices "Save and Spend":

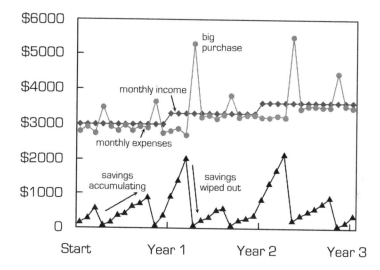

Take a close look at it. The Monthly Income for this person starts at $3,000 (that is, they make $36,000/year). The first month, their expenses were $2,800, so they saved $200, which shows up as the Accumulated Savings for the first month. The next month, they earned $3,000 and spent $2,900, so they save only $100 that month—but that adds to the $200 they had from last month, so their accumulated savings goes up to $300. In the third month, they earn $3,000 and spend only $2,700, thus saving $300 that month, so their accumulated savings goes up from $300 to $600. Up to now they've been saving and doing quite a nice job of it.

But suddenly, that $600 in their saving account starts to look pretty juicy. We're tired of that small TV, and our favorite store has a sale on Wide-screen TVs for $599—what a coincidence! Let's buy one!

So, the next month, they spend the usual $2,800 on regular expenses, plus buy the TV for $600—resulting in $3,400 expenses that month, thus wiping out their savings. Then they save for a few more months, accumulating nicely up to $1,000, and then wipe it all out by buying new bedroom furniture. Notice that each big purchase has the effect of wiping out the savings. Notice also that the big purchases happen when the savings get to a certain size. It's common for people to have a "magic number"—when their savings gets bigger than that number, they start feeling like they really need to buy something big with it. The common expression for this is "the money is burning a hole in my pocket."

This spending pattern is exactly what many children are taught to do, with the "Piggy-Bank and Allowance" method of financial education. We are taught to work for our money (by the allowance) and then taught to **save** it (in the piggy bank) until the savings are big enough to **purchase** something cool. Then we start the process over again.

There's something else evident in the graph. Notice that after a year, the person's income goes from $3,000/month to $3,300/month—a 10 percent raise. At first, they keep their spending at the previous level—somewhere around $2,700/month. But because their income has gone up and their expenses stayed the same, their savings start to accumulate at a really great rate. This can only mean one thing—time to spend! But now, it takes a *really* big purchase to wipe out the savings, like maybe a big vacation. And, when they get back from vacation, they've bought some goodies on credit cards and have to pay those off, so their expenses go up too. Magically, the expenses go up just enough so that the person is back to saving a few hundred dollars each month.

So, what does the raise get you? Some travel, some new toys, an empty bank account, and higher expectations and expenses. In the next chapter, we will see how to avoid the trap of regularly depleting your savings.

Confusing Saving and Investing

The third trap has to do with confusing Saving and Investing. Most of us were taught by the Piggy-Bank method that we were supposed to save. And then, as a teenager, when we got our first bank account, we learn that we will get interest on our savings, and that interest can grow in a compound way. That subtle step causes us to think of our savings account as the place where investing happens—after all, it's earning interest, right?

Here is an important distinction to make: The piggy-bank type of saving that we learned to do is really **deferred spending**, not investing. If it's in your savings account, you will use it to save *for some later large purchase.* That is very different from investing, or accumulating capital for the purpose of investing, and it is important that you know when you are **saving** and when you are **investing**. In the next chapter, you will see that accumulating capital for investing purposes really requires a different account in a different institution. If you try to use your savings account for this purpose, it just won't work, because you won't be able to protect your investment capital when the time comes to buy the things you've been saving for.

Buying Expense-Generating Possessions

The fourth financial trap is buying expense-generating possessions. When we buy a car, house, skis, etc. we need to realize that these possessions will trigger new expenses, beyond the initial purchase price. When you are deciding how much car you can afford, and the salesman is leading you away from the

Honda Civic sedan toward the Lexus, remember that it's not just the down payments and the monthly payments you have to cope with. You also have to deal with sales tax, licensing fees, insurance, smog checks, gas, oil, maintenance, etc. No-one is there to remind you of that when you gulp and agree to the fancier, nicer car—but there will be a lot of people waiting to take your money once the car is in your garage. Choose a car and a house that will allow you to live below your means!

Failing to Learn to Invest Beyond House

The fifth financial trap has to do with complacency and lack of financial education: failing to learn to invest beyond house. A common Middle Class expression is "My home is my greatest asset." If that statement is true for your whole life, then you have missed the opportunity to invest beyond your home, and probably you will have put all of your financial resources into the largest home you could afford, rather than the smallest home that would meet your needs, thus minimizing the triggered expenses associated with your home.

Confusing Investing and Gambling

The sixth financial trap has to do with carelessness and lack of awareness of what it takes to make a good investment. There *are* good investments out there, but they are found hidden in a sea of bad investments. The only way to tell a good one from a bad one is to have been watching them all for a while, to know the market you're playing in, and to really be quantitative about it. Why do you think that stock is going to go up? Just because it seems to have some momentum? Because your friend says it's hot? Or is it because you have read their prospectus, estimated the number of customers the company should be able to acquire with their new products, estimated the earnings per customer, and then can compute the expected earnings of the company, which at the present price-to-earnings ratio would imply a new share price which is that much higher than the current price? If you can't justify what you think the share price of the company should be, you're just gambling, and you are likely to lose. If you want to actually make money in the stock market, much less actually beat the broad indices, you will need to take a very research-oriented and quantitative approach to it. I recommend Peter Lynch's *Beating the Street* to see how to execute the quantitative approach. If you are new to playing the market, play small and don't trade on margin (that is, don't trade with borrowed money), so you will not get hurt too badly if it goes against you.   My experience with the stock market so far has been that I break even—I've done much better in rental real estate, technology licensing, and stock options in a company I worked for that was subsequently acquired by a larger company.   Note that the warning about gambling on margin also applies to real estate—the subprime mortgage crisis is a spectacular example of the improper use of debt to speculate on real estate, which actually fueled a dangerous market bubble.

Why We Fall for the Traps

So, the traps are all fairly obvious once you take a look at them, and in fact, you may have been intellectually aware that you were taking action that was not good for you financially, but was satisfying on some other level—enough so that it seemed worthwhile to compromise your long-term financial future. There are some properties of being human that are the basis for the financial traps.

The Need for Status

In *The Moral Animal*, Robert Wright presents compelling evidence of the importance of social status in human societies. High social standing confers upon us greater access to food, preferred shelter and sexual opportunity. Wealth is highly correlated with status, for both sexes but especially for men.

Physical attractiveness is also correlated with status, for both sexes but especially for women.

The good news is: the need for status that seems to be built into us is a large factor in our desire to be wealthy. We realize that wealth will make our lives more secure and enjoyable, and the desire for wealth causes us to work hard and leads to increased productivity for us personally and as a society.

It used to be that the only way to *look* high-status was to actually *be* high-status. In a society based on hunting prowess or some other skill or personal attributes, you were quickly discovered if you didn't have the necessary skill. But something has happened in our modern society, with modern financial instruments, including credit cards: it is possible to look higher-status than you really are, by borrowing money against your future earnings, and then buying flashy possessions like cars, homes, jewelry, etc.

So, if we are not careful, our *desire for status* leads to a *desire to look wealthy even if we aren't*, which is at the root of several of the financial traps (borrowing to buy possessions, saving only to buy possessions, buying expense-generating possessions). Would you want to *be* wealthy if it meant that, for a while, you couldn't *look* wealthy? Read *The Millionaire Next Door* to learn more about how many wealthy people kept their lifestyles modest while they grew their wealth (and then *keep* their wealth by keeping their lifestyles modest).

The Need for Immediate Gratification

Closely related to the need for status is the need for immediate gratification. Why should we wait to acquire status when we can borrow now and attain the appearance of status? This immediate attainment of status via acquired debt hurts us terribly in the long run but can be extremely satisfying in the short run. The need for immediate gratification is a factor in several financial traps (borrowing to buy possessions, saving only to buy possessions, confusing saving and investing, and confusing investing and gambling).

Weak Financial Education—Piggy-Bank and Allowance

Our weak financial education, based on the Piggy-Bank and Allowance, is the direct training in the Save and Spend habit. It may help us to remember why we train our children with the piggy-bank and allowance, because in fact, they aren't all bad. The purpose of the allowance was to teach us that money doesn't come for free, that it has to be worked for. The purpose of the piggy bank was to help us develop the ability to delay gratification. Both of these lessons serve a useful purpose in our financial education and in building our character.

The problem is that the financial education shouldn't stop there. The next step is in teaching of the value of accumulating capital *not for the purpose of spending* but for the purpose of providing for one's future survival.

Weak Financial Education—Fear of Numbers

The fear of numbers is a factor in all of the financial traps. It is a sad fact that many people find math frustrating and irritating. It turns out the arithmetic required to understand the process of financial independence is really quite simple. If you can add and subtract, and you know *what* to add and subtract, you're most of the way there.

Robert Kiyosaki has developed the best solution I have ever seen for teaching the necessary accounting skills. It is his *Cash Flow* board game, which allows you to simulate the process of achieving financial independence. In the process of playing this fun game, you keep track of your income and expenses, while you acquire investments, purchase possessions, and have children (thus increasing your expenses), all the while attempting to increase your passive income until it equals your expenses. When you achieve this goal, you are "out of the Rat Race", and entitled to play on a new section of the board, that simulates the life of the wealthy. This game is truly a stroke of genius and I highly recommend it. It is expensive (about $200) but worth every penny. You can order it at www.richdad.com.

Feeling Entitled to Stop Learning

The arresting of the learning process is a factor in all of the financial traps. A strange thing happens when people leave school, either by graduating or dropping out. Most people act as though the learning phase of their lives is over, and, with their education soundly behind them, they plunge into the exhausting world of working for living.

To take this attitude is to misunderstand the learning process, and also to misunderstand the world in which we live. Learning is something that can take place throughout a lifetime, both in and out of school. And, on top of that, the world is changing so fast now that just about everything you learned 5 years ago is obsolete anyway. The only way to survive and prosper is to keep learning as you go, for the rest of your life.

Financial education is not taught in schools, for a variety of reasons. That means that you have to seek out your financial teachers and role models, and learn about this fascinating subject *independently* of your conventional education. Recognize that you have at least three types of education:

1. General Education
2. Professional Education
3. Financial Education

And they are all different. The fact that you have read this far means you are working diligently on your Financial Education. See the reference list at the end of the book for other interesting and valid points of view.

Fear of Risk

The fear of risk is a factor in the trap of failing to learn to invest beyond house. In *Beating the Street*, Peter Lynch wrote,

> "I'm convinced that it's the cultural memory of the 1929 Crash more than any other single factor that continues to keep millions of investors away from stocks and attracts them to bonds and to money-market accounts."

Similar statements could be made about real estate investing, since real estate markets also have had large and sudden drops, as in the recent 2008 real estate crash. Increased risk is associated with higher returns, so if you want higher performance in your investments, you will need to develop some risk tolerance, while still being prudent about debt exposure.

Abdicating Financial Responsibility in a Relationship

This is a difficult area to discuss, but it can be a major factor in married couples falling into all of the traps. Succeeding financially requires initiative and an ability to take ownership of one's financial education. But often, one person in a relationship will defer to the other for all matters associated with money. This can rob one person of their education, while making the other person feel overly responsible and risk-averse. The net result can be a kind of mutual financial paralysis—neither party develops their financial abilities and gains experience with investing and business. I have seen relationships in which both parties were financially paralyzed until the relationship ended, and then both took the initiative and became extremely interested in their own financial future.

Fear of Wealth or Limiting Beliefs about Money

Money and Wealth are emotionally charged subjects. At one level, we may desire money and wealth, so that we can enjoy our lives and provide for our needs—but at another level, we may feel that the accumulation of wealth is selfish, or not want to succeed beyond a parent; perhaps you know someone who is financially successful but has other personality traits that you don't like, and so you have associated wealth with those negative traits. These negative emotions and beliefs about money can lead to self-sabotage, and really hold us back in succeeding financially.

Difficulty with Sustained and Intermittent Effort

It takes time to build up your financial education, and it takes time to execute your plan to grow your wealth. But the actions are often intermittent—we may have intense periods where we are buying a rental property, for example, then breaks while our capital is tied up and we are waiting for the next opportunity. The intermittent quality of this effort makes it difficult for us—once we shift our focus to something else, it may be hard to remember to shift it back.

Now that we have looked at the financial traps, and looked at the reasons we fall into them, it is time to look at the personal attributes that we can develop that will allow us to avoid the traps, and then map out the path to financial independence.

Part III

The Path to Financial Independence

The Path to Financial Independence

Now that we understand how time and money work, what the financial traps are, and why we fall into them, we are in a position to understand the path to Financial Independence.

Attitudes that Lead to Financial Independence

Just as there are psychological reasons for falling into the financial traps, there are personal attitudes that will enable you to successfully travel the path to Financial Independence.

Lack of Need for External Indications of Status

If you are going to become wealthy, rather than just look wealthy, you are going to need to live below your means so you can accumulate capital for the purpose of investing and creating businesses. That will mean that, as you are on the path, you won't want to spend money on the things that will make you look wealthy, like fancy new cars, a large home, expensive jewelry, etc. I have found that a quiet inner confidence begins to develop as you know you are growing your wealth and you are on the path. This inner source of strength is much more satisfying than the external indications of status.

In the year 2000, I drove a 1987 Mazda RX-7 that I bought used in 1994 for $5,000. I really liked this little car, but it was not a flashy status car—I could have afforded a much more expensive car, but then I wouldn't have had that money to invest and give me options while I grew my new business. In 2004, when I had raised $5 Million in venture capital financing for my business, I bought a Kia Amanti for $25,000 - it seemed like a huge step up, but in fact I was still carefully living well below my means.

When you are feeling concerned about your image and your status, here's a saying that can help you put it in perspective: "We would worry much less about what people think of us if we knew just how seldom they do." Most people will respect your frugality and intelligence, especially when they see that you are doing creative and profitable things with the money you aren't wasting on flashy frills. And when they realize that you are headed for real wealth—watch what happens to your status then!

Ability to Defer Gratification

Related to the above discussion is the ability to defer gratification. When you feel the urge to buy some flashy new toy, instead of satisfying that urge immediately, ask, "How can I create the money for it?" Use it as a reward for the effort involved in activating your financial genius and creating some new wealth.

I do make an important exception to this guideline, however. If the thing I desire is a tool that is necessary to help me learn a skill, I will usually act very decisively and get it right away. In this case, I consider it an investment in my education and my life assets to have the new skill, and I tend to not skimp or delay. One example would be the software that allows me to edit images for my web pages. I realized in 1994 that the web would be huge and I had better learn how to make web pages, so I immediately bought the tools I needed to do the job. The ability to make nice-looking websites really fast has paid for itself a thousandfold and opened up doors for me that I didn't even know existed.

Strong Financial Education

To succeed financially, you will need to have a strong financial education, that includes the ability to manage your cash flow, the ability to read a company prospectus, understand taxes, corporations, etc. When I got my first job, I took a correspondence course called "Successful Investing and Money Management", and learned all about taxes, balance sheets, etc. Be proactive and seek out financial knowledge from whatever source you can find. Read the books in the reading list at the back of this book.

No Fear of Numbers and Accounting

Eliminating the fear of numbers and accounting is obviously related to getting a strong financial education, but may be deeper than that. In general, you will want to make investments that produce positive cash flow. For example, in a rental income property, the cash flow will be the difference between the rental income and the expenses, which will include monthly mortgage payment, property taxes, maintenance costs, insurance, etc. The cash flow will end up being a *small difference of large numbers*, which may be positive or negative.   Your ability to keep the costs down and monitor them carefully will determine whether this investment is an asset (producing positive cash flow) or an expense-generator (producing negative cash flow). To win at this game, you will need to enjoy being precise about cash flow, and that will mean being fluent with the numbers and being willing to work with them like an accountant. Consider playing Robert Kiyosaki's Cash Flow game (available at www. richdad.com) to get practice in tracking your income, expenses, assets and liabilities.

Commitment to Lifetime Learning

Developing your financial intelligence is a commitment to keep learning, for two reasons: 1) There is a huge amount out there already to learn, and 2) it keeps changing and evolving anyway. Successful people keep an open mind and are always excited about learning something new.

Ability to Manage Risk

Investments with high growth potential always carry with them the risk of some kind of loss. You will have to be able to cope with this risk, and arrange your investments accordingly. This is the reason that I recommend a "base layer" of stable, low-risk investments, then as your capital grows, you can assume higher risk on your later money.

Healthy Financial Responsibility in a Relationship

If you are in a financial relationship with someone (for example, if you are married, or living with someone in a common-law state), then you have linked your finances together. Have you talked about your plans to grow your wealth? Are you linked to someone who is much more financially educated than you are (if so, you need to get educated), or is less financially educated than you are (if so, you need to help them get educated)? Have you considered the ramifications of a dissolution of the relationship? This is an area where "my home is my biggest asset" can really hurt you. If it is your only asset, and you need to dissolve your relationship, you will be faced with a serious problem: probably one person will want to stay in the house (often with the children) while the other person will want to sell or refinance the house to get half the equity out. If there are no other assets to negotiate with, this situation is a serious problem. This suggests strongly that living below your means, buying less house than you can afford, and having money left over to invest is a healthy strategy. But adopting this strategy will require financial education and cooperation between both parties, and, perhaps most importantly of all, a realization that both people need to preserve their own financial integrity within the relationship.

Acceptance of Wealth

Wealthy people welcome wealth into their lives. We seek it out, because we believe we have a right to enjoy the good things that life has to offer. And we understand that other people can make different choices, and may have their own attitudes about money, and there is nothing we can do about that. It is important to get in touch with your attitudes about money. Do you believe you are entitled to having wealth in your life? How much wealth? Do you have any reservations? Maybe you feel you are entitled to *this much* but not *that much*. Is there a wealth level at which you would feel uncomfortable? Why? Do you have relatives or friends whose expectations of you are placing a limitation on you? They are entitled to think what they want, but only you can decide if you will accept those limitations. Casting them off is easy if you realize they are projections from other people onto you. But casting them off is impossible if you actually believe them yourself. Do you have any negative associations with wealth? Perhaps you know someone who is very money-conscious, but talks too much about it. Realize that you can welcome wealth into your life, while still maintaining your sense of discretion.

Here's another interesting metaphysical look at the acceptance of wealth. If there is something you desire in your life, but it is not coming in, even though you wish for it, ask yourself, "Have I created a place for it to go?" Many people wish for wealth, while only maintaining a savings and a chequing account. That is exactly like holding out a leaky bucket and wishing for water to accumulate. You need to give it a non-leaky place to go!

Similarly, if you have something in your life that you wish you could get rid of, but it just won't go away, ask yourself, "Have I given it a place to hide?" Your credit card balance on several credit cards is a great place for consumer debt to hide. You have created this hiding place, and now the debt lurks there with your permission. Open the windows, let the light in, expose these hiding demons and shoo them out for good!

Ability to make Sustained and Intermittent Effort

The process of reaching financial independence takes time—many enjoyable years of continued learning, and exciting and profitable challenges. Reaching your goals will require effort to be sustained for a long time, yet it will often be intermittent. You will need to have a way to keep your mind sharp and aware of where you are in the process, even when you are not in the middle of a related action. In the next chapter, I will offer my approach for keeping long-term focus with intermittent action.

The Stages on the Path to Financial Independence

Now, we will look at the stages on the path to Financial Independence. In my view, there are four different stages on the path:

1. Youth/Education
2. Accumulate Capital / Conservative investing
3. Small Deals
4. Big Deals and Corporations / Brokering Deals

In addition to these four stages, there are two traps:

1. Borrow and Spend
2. Save and Spend

These stages and traps can be visualized by their effect on your net worth as you age, as shown in the figure below. There are things you need to do to succeed in each stage, and there are things you can be doing to prepare for the next stage before you get to it. Using this figure as a guide, I will outline the properties of each of the stages and traps, and what the necessary actions are in each one.

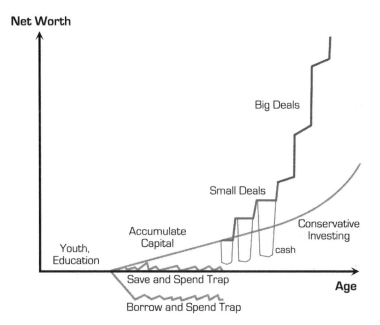

The Stages on the Path to Financial Independence

Stage One—Youth/Education

In this stage, we are just starting out in life. We have no net worth to speak of (unless an inheritance is on the horizon), and our only assets are our Life Assets—our education, health, relationships, organization and habits. This is the stage of life to cultivate these Life Assets. The stronger the foundation at this stage, the easier it will be later to build a skyscraper of wealth and personal achievement. Most people at this stage will not have credit cards, so they haven't accumulated consumer debt yet. But, some people may have significant student loans.

Actions and Habits to Develop:

1. **Complete general and professional education to your highest potential.** Work hard at school and do as well as you can. Learn what your teachers are saying, but think for yourself and develop the habit of questioning authority. Does your teacher's instruction apply to your particular situation? How would you modify it to account for your life circumstances? How would you teach it if you had a student? Some of my best insights have come from a feeling of dissatisfaction with something I was taught—*there must be a better way to teach this!* When I look for those things, I always end up with some kind of an explanation, or a diagram, that makes the relationships clear or unambiguous.

    This entire book is an example of that. I read and benefited greatly from Robert Kiyosaki's book *Rich Dad, Poor Dad* (and I recommend it highly to you)—but I was troubled by his discussion about Assets and Liabilities, because he was re-defining the meaning of the words in terms of cash flow. I could see the great wisdom in what he was saying, I just found his phrasing of the idea to be confusing. That dissatisfaction caused me to develop my flow diagrams and get clear about expense-generating possessions, which are two of the primary ideas in this book.

2. **Raise your earning potential as high as possible.** It will be so much easier to accumulate capital in the next step if your income is high (and you have kept your expenses low).

3. **Invest heavily in your financial education.** Remember that you have three different kinds of education: General education, Professional education, and Financial education. Your general education and professional education will raise your earning potential, but your financial education will make it possible for you to go beyond "working for a living" to "making your money work for you." The books I read that I consider the foundation of my financial education were *The Richest Man in Babylon, Your Money or Your Life,* and *Rich Dad, Poor Dad,* as well as a correspondence course by Hume Publishing entitled *Successful Investing and Money Management.* I also consider Kiyosaki's Cash Flow game a vital part of my financial education and I recommend it highly. References are given at the end of this book.

4. **Keep your expenses low.** Develop the habit of living below your means. If you can do it when your income is low, think how easy it will be when your income is high after you graduate.

5. **Avoid consumer debt.** Similar to the above, don't get sucked into the consumer debt trap. There are highly paid sales reps canvassing on college campuses, signing up students for credit cards. Why are they trying so hard to get you into a credit card? They are trying to lure you into the "Borrow and Spend" trap, so that when you get your first job, you will be primed to start buying on credit. Don't fall for it. Respect yourself and your financial future. Avoid consumer debt at all costs. If you do use a card for its convenience, *always* pay it off every month. Never make such a large purchase that you actually are borrowing money from your credit card company—that's a loan at 19 percent!!

6. **Pay Yourself First 10 percent.**   This is the classic formula (from *The Richest Man in Babylon*) for accumulating capital that you can then use to invest. If you do this, you will by definition be living below your means.
7. **Get on-line.** If you haven't already, learn how to use email and how to surf the web.

Trap One—Borrow and Spend

If you find yourself in this trap, then it means that you have developed the habit of accumulating debt to purchase possessions (or possibly to finance your education).

Actions and Habits to Develop:

1. **Eliminate the possibility of accumulating any more debt.** The old saying goes, "If you find yourself in a hole, stop digging." This means: tear up your credit cards, right now.
2. **Pay off the debt with 20 percent of your income.** The classic formula (given in *The Richest Man in Babylon*) for paying off the debt is to set aside 20 percent of your take-home pay for debt repayment, 10 percent to pay yourself into your investing account, and 70 percent to live on. If you have more than one credit card, look at the interest rates that are being charged, and pay off the cards with the highest interest rate first (while still making the minimum payments on the others). You may want to consult a financial planner or consumer debt consolidation agency if your debts are severe. They are listed in my Yellow Pages *under Credit & Debt Counseling Services*—most of them are non-profit community service organizations. One of the services they provide is to negotiate on your behalf with your creditors. I called one service and they said that most credit card companies will automatically reduce your interest rate from 19 percent to 9.9 percent when they become involved in representing you. You may be able to renegotiate your rate independently, too.

    If 20 percent of your income is not enough to make your interest payments, you are in a financial emergency and should seek qualified financial counseling immediately.
3. **Invest heavily in your financial education.** (repeated from Stage One—Youth/Education) Remember that you have three different kinds of education: General education,

Professional education, and Financial education. Your general education and professional education will raise your earning potential, but your financial education will make it possible for you to go beyond "working for a living" to "making your money work for you." The books I read that I consider the foundation of my financial education were *The Richest Man in Babylon, Your Money or Your Life,* and *Rich Dad, Poor Dad,* as well as a correspondence course by Hume Publishing entitled *Successful Investing and Money Management.* I also consider Kiyosaki's Cash Flow game a vital part of my financial education and I recommend it highly. References are given at the end of this book.

4. **Keep your expenses low.** You will be living on 70 percent of your income, which will presumably require you to reduce your expenses for a while.

5. **Pay Yourself First 10 percent.** This is the classic formula (from *The Richest Man in Babylon*) for accumulating capital that you can then use to invest. If you do this, you will by definition be living below your means.

6. **Get on-line.** (Repeated from Stage One—Youth/Education) If you haven't already, learn how to use email and how to surf the web.

Trap Two—Save and Spend

If you find yourself in this trap, then it means that you have developed the habit of saving to purchase possessions, but without accumulating capital for investing purposes.

Actions and Habits to Develop:

1. **Create an investing account for your capital to accumulate.** You probably already have a chequing account and a saving account, but I'm talking about a *third* account for your investing account. And it should be at a different institution than your other bank accounts. This is because we want to make sure there is no way for money to leak out of your investing account into your other accounts. Your investing account will be the physical embodiment of your "cup"—the leaky bucket is represented by your two bank accounts. I personally use a Schwab account for my investing account, for several reasons:
   - It is a different institution from my bank, so there is no chance of hidden transfers (like overdraft protection).
   - They have a good on-line presence, so I can check my balances and execute trades quickly via the Internet.
   - They have branch offices everywhere, so I can easily drive down there, hand them a cheque, and make a transaction immediately. Other discount on-line brokerage services don't have the branch offices, so you have to mail a cheque to them which can take days to get into the system.
   - They have many safeguards designed to protect people from overly aggressive trading, such as not allowing margin on certain volatile stocks.

   You can find Schwab on the Internet at www.schwab.com. Other online brokers include Datek (www.datek.com), E-trade (www.etrade.com), Ameritrade (www.ameritrade.com), etc. The others have lower trading fees, but lack the advantage of the branch offices and other in-person services near you.

2. **Set up regular transfers into your new investing account at 10 percent.** Pay yourself first 10 percent—get the computers to do it for you.

3. **Invest heavily in your financial education.** (repeated from Stage One—Youth/Education) Remember that you have three different kinds of education: General education, Professional education, and Financial education. Your general education and professional education will raise your earning potential, but your financial education will make it possible for you to go beyond "working for a living" to "making your money work for you." The books I read that I consider the foundation of my financial education were *The Richest Man in Babylon, Your Money or Your Life,* and *Rich Dad, Poor Dad,* as well as a correspondence course by Hume Publishing entitled *Successful Investing and Money Management.* I also consider Kiyosaki's Cash Flow game a vital part of my financial education and I recommend it highly. References are given at the end of this book.

4. **Keep your expenses low.**

Stage Two—Accumulate Capital for Conservative Investing

In this stage, we have avoided the two traps of "Save and Spend" and "Borrow and Spend", have established an investment account, are living debt-free below our means, and are in the process of accumulating capital for investment purposes. Great! This is a fabulous foundation on which to build.

If your plan is to stay long-term with low-effort investments, such as mutual funds, then simply continue to make your regular contributions of 10 percent of your income into your investing account, work with a financial planner you respect, and let time and compound interest work their magic for you. This is the standard upper-middle-class approach to wealth accumulation and can do very well, especially if you start young enough.

Here's how it can work. In this spreadsheet example, I have assumed that you accumulate capital by putting aside 10 percent of your take-home pay into an aggressive growth mutual fund that averages 2 percent/month return, or a 26.8 percent annual return. Yes, I know that's very high—but then, the INVESCO Technology Fund averaged 25.7 percent/year over the 10 years from 1990-2000. Don't worry, this is just an example so you will be able to see some relationships you may not have seen before—shortly I'll discuss how to make it work even with a low rate of return.

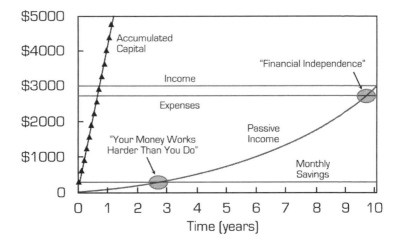

In this figure, I assume that the person has a $3,000/month after-tax **income**. 90 percent of her income, or $2,700/month goes toward her **expenses**. She puts 10 percent of it (her **monthly savings** of $300) each month into her investing account, and doesn't ever take it out, so her **accumulated capital** starts to grow nicely and goes off the chart. Can you see that it starts at $300 in the first month, and goes up steadily at the rate of $300 each passing month? The **passive income**, or return on the accumulated capital is shown on the bottom of the chart. At first, the return is quite small, but as the capital accumulates by her regular contributions and by the compound interest, her return each month becomes larger, too. Just before the third year, her passive income grows to the point where it crosses over and exceeds the monthly savings - at this point, her money is producing more income than she is putting away - "Your Money works Harder than You Do." Finally, just before the tenth year, her monthly return reaches $2,700/month. But that is equal to her expenses—so now, she could carefully liquidate a small fraction of her accumulated capital, and live off the growth, no longer needing to work. This magic point is what

Joe Dominguez and Vicki Robin called the "Crossover Point" in *Your Money or Your Life*. In *Rich Dad, Poor Dad*, Robert Kiyosaki calls it "Getting Out of the Rat Race." Whatever you want to call it, it is the point at which your money (accumulated capital) is producing enough return for you to live on.

So, earlier I said, don't worry that I have chosen such a high return rate, because I just wanted you to see that the crossover point does exist. You can get a similar crossover to occur even with a low return. Dominguez and Robin recommend putting your money into government Treasury Bills, a guaranteed investment with a low return rate around 6 percent, and saving more than 10 percent of your income, simply by really getting in touch with your true spending needs. They show an example in *Your Money or Your Life* of a person who saved more like 50 percent of his income and invested it at a 6 percent return and hit the crossover point in about 5 years. Play with the numbers yourself in a spreadsheet—you will be amazed at the effect of reducing your expenses. Lowering your expenses has two effects on the charts: it gives you more capital to accumulate each month, and it lowers the target you have to reach to cross over. The further you live below your means, the faster you get out of the Rat Race.

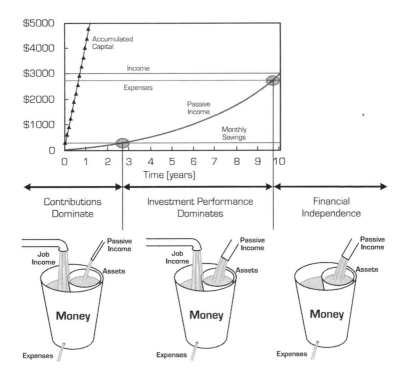

In this next figure, I am showing the progression along with the flow diagrams from the first chapter. Notice that the figure is divided up into three regions: an early stage in which *Contributions Dominate*, a middle stage in which *Investment Performance Dominates*, and the final stage of *Financial Independence*.

In the early stage, approximately the first three years, the passive income is smaller than the monthly savings—that is, your money is growing mostly because you are keeping what you make, not so much because of your great rate of return. In this first few years, your *contributions dominate*—that is, your discipline in putting money in and not taking it out is the dominant effect in your accumulating capital. You have to accumulate some money before it can work for you.

But at about the third year, the passive income crosses over the monthly savings line. That is, after the third year, your money is growing mostly because of the return on your investment, and less and less because you are socking it away. For the next seven years, your *Investment Performance Dominates.* That is, your money is now working harder for you than you are!

Finally, at about the tenth year, the passive income crosses over the monthly expenses line, and that is where your money is strong enough to pay your expenses for you. At this stage, you have become financially independent, and no longer need the job income to live at that lifestyle.

Neat, eh? Now you may not have noticed something, but there is a very reassuring message contained in this figure. A lot of people feel that they can't start on an investing program because they don't know enough to get a high return. This figure makes it clear that, at first, the most important thing is to put it away and not take it out—*Contributions Dominate.* You have several years to learn about getting a high rate of return. In the first three years, accumulate capital while you educate yourself on how to get a good return. Your investment performance only becomes dominant in years 3-10. So, go easy on yourself when you're starting out, you don't have to be Warren Buffett right away!

One last interesting thing. Remember the formula for Survival Time in the first chapter? In this case, it would be Assets/ (Expenses–Passive Income). We can compute that, and here's what it looks like:

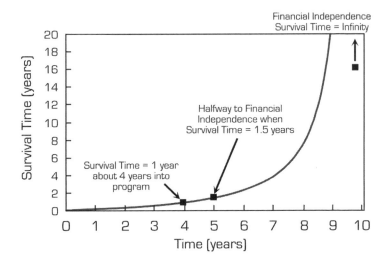

The first thing is to notice that the survival time goes up to infinity when the Passive Income equals the expenses—that's when you get out of the Rat Race. The survival time is about 1 year, when you are about 4 years into the program. The survival time is about 1.5 years when you are about half-way through the program. So, that's a pretty good rule of thumb. When your survival time is about eighteen months, you're about half-way to being financially independent.

Actions and Habits to Develop:

1. **Cultivate a relationship with a good financial planner.** Good advice is worth paying for. Your financial planner can help you get a good return on your investment earlier than you would on your own. And they can help you see problems and opportunities you might otherwise miss.
2. **Keep your expenses low.**
3. **Continue to avoid consumer debt.**

4. **Continue to Pay Yourself First 10 percent.** Continue to accumulate capital and let your money grow in your mutual fund account.

5. **Get on-line.** If you haven't already, learn how to use email and how to surf the web. This will allow you to keep in touch easily with your financial planner and other financially savvy friends, and let you track your investment portfolio on-line.

Stage Two—Accumulate Capital for Aggressive Investing

In this stage, we have avoided the two traps of "Save and Spend" and "Borrow and Spend", have established an investment account, are living debt-free below our means, and are in the process of accumulating capital for investment purposes. Great! This is a fabulous foundation on which to build.

If you choose to take a more aggressive approach, and are willing to put in more time and effort to reap the potential rewards, here are the next steps:

Actions and Habits to Develop:

1. **Learn about Small Deals by playing Kiyosaki's Cash Flow game.** This amazing teaching tool will give you simulated experience in evaluating investment and business opportunities. Should I buy the stock of that utility company, with its fixed price and fixed yield of 10 percent, or should I wait for that 2-bedroom 1-bath condominium, costing $40,000 with a down payment of $4,000 and a positive cash flow of $140/month and the possibility of selling later between $45,000 and $65,000?

2. **Educate yourself in the type of deals you want to do.** If you want to buy rental property, then start going to open houses, reading the paper, taking courses in foreclosure financing, making connections with bankruptcy attorneys, networking with people you know who are successful in making deals like this. I highly recommend John T. Reed's books on real estate investing (references at the end of this book). If you want to invest in businesses, start looking at the business-for-sale section of the paper, talking to people who own businesses in your neighborhood or in a growth area nearby. Take some time to prepare for your first deals and understand the prevailing market conditions, so you can notice when things change and create opportunities.

3. **Start lining up sources of financing.** Many of the kinds of deals you will want to do will require financing of some kind. For example, if you want to buy a rental property, you will want to put up the smallest down payment you can, and finance the rest at the most favorable rate possible. Start creating your relationships with people or institutions who can lend you the money to make your investment.

   Don't necessarily assume that the outside money has to come from a bank or mortgage lender. You may have a relative, friend, or business associate who might participate with you in the deal if you structure it in a suitably businesslike way. Talk to your trusted elders and let them know you are getting ready to make a deal and you are looking for financing. You might be surprised that they want to help you get started.

   This is how I financed my first house purchase—not by a gift, but by an investment by my father, who put in $60,000 into a $120,000 house purchase. We structured his investment as a capital gain, not a loan, and so I didn't have to make a monthly payment to him for the three years I held the house. I lived in the house for 10 months and then went to grad school in the U.S., so I rented the house out for $1100/month for nearly three years, which paid my rent in the states, while I got valuable experience being an absentee landlord. When I sold the house for $210,000 a few years later, he got $73,500, representing a 7 percent annual compound return on his money over three years, treated as a capital gain, which (at that time, for him, in Canada) was tax-free because of the $250,000 lifetime capital gains exemption. The rest of the gain went to me, also tax-free for the same reason. So you see that a little creative financing allowed me to put together a deal with great cash flow, and created a benefit both to me and to my father in a well-structured deal.

By the way, the really funny part of this deal was explaining it to my dad's accountant, who really seemed to have trouble understanding it. Awaken your financial genius and find a way to make your deal happen!

4. **Keep your expenses low.**
5. **Continue to avoid consumer debt.**
6. **Continue to Pay Yourself First 10 percent.**
7. **Get on-line.** If you haven't already, learn how to use email and how to surf the web.

Stage Three—Small Deals

In this stage, we have avoided the two traps of "Save and Spend" and "Borrow and Spend", have established an investment account, are living debt-free below our means, and have accumulated enough capital to be able to make some Small Deals. This is where life starts to get really interesting!

Here's what a Small Deal looks like from a financial point of view. In general, a deal will contain the following elements:

- A down payment
- Some financing required and an associated liability
- Some initial cash flow, which may change over the life of the investment
- An expected sale price range at some future date
- Expected closing costs

Every deal is different, and part of the fun is coming up with creative advantages for the particular situation you are in. This is where your financial genius can be awakened. If you do conventional deals, you'll get average returns; and if you do special deals, you may get special returns.

Let's say you have accumulated $10,000 in your investing account and are looking for your first Small Deal. You decide that a small real estate deal might be right for you, say, a 2-bedroom 1-bathroom townhouse in an area with good growth potential. It can be purchased for $40,000, with a down payment of $4,000, incurring a real estate liability of $36,000. But you discover that after financing the property and some minor cosmetic renovations, you can rent it out for a little more than the monthly mortgage and taxes, resulting in a small positive cash flow of +$40/month, or $480/year, or an annual return on investment of 480/4000 = 12 percent. After a year, you raise the rent by $80, so your cash flow goes up to +$120/month, or $1440/year, for an annual return on investment of 1440/4000 = 36 percent, and then at the end of the second year, you notice that the growth in the area means you can offer it for sale at $57,000—after the real estate agent takes 7 percent, leaving you with $53,000, a profit of $13,000 with a $4,000 investment. So, here's what the deal looked like in picture form:

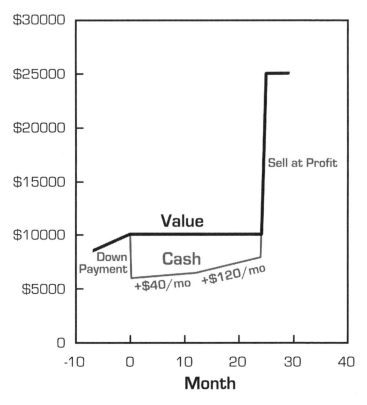

You start with your $10,000 in cash in your investing account. You buy the property by putting down $4,000, depleting your cash to $6000. Your cash then rises in the first year at +$40/ month, then rises more steeply in the second year at +$120/ month. Then you sell the property, getting back your down payment and making a profit of $13,000. Notice that you end up with about $25,000, which is the $10,000 you started with, plus the total cash flow for the two years of $1,920, plus the profit of $13,000, for a total of $24,920.

Now, this is a sweet little deal. You got a nice little cash flow, and made a profit, and it wasn't that much work being the landlord for a couple of years. (I've done it and it's not so bad!)

Beware, though, not all deals are this rosy. Sometimes tenants refuse to pay rent and you have to evict them (I had to do this). You lose a couple months' rent in the process. Or, it might not be possible to have the property be cash flow positive in the first year, but you might decide to buy it anyway—in that case, you better make sure you have enough cash on hand to cover the expected losses. Remember, the cash flow is a small difference of large numbers, and if one of those numbers changes, your cash flow can be seriously affected.

So, the up-front need for cash for the down payment, and the possibility of negative cash flow, mean that you need to have a certain amount of cash before you can even consider getting into deals like this. That's why I am showing Capital Accumulation as a necessary step before you graduate to Small Deals. You need cash, and you need the education and skills to manage cash flow before you start making deals like this.

Now, just because I used real estate as an example, doesn't mean that's the only kind of Small Deal you can do. There are also entrepreneurial and business Small Deals, starting a little company and selling it, etc. They all involve risk, they all involve cash up front and good management of cash flow, and they all can return very big if you do things right and have your wits about you. Play Kiyosaki's Cash Flow game if you want to see more examples of juicy Small Deals.

The trick is then to take the new money from your first sweet little deal, and use it to make the down payment on your second sweet little deal. So, maybe the second deal looks like a 3-bedroom 2-bathroom house in an area you expect to grow, selling for $120,000, requiring a down payment of $12,000, with the possibility to sell 3 years later for $210,000 (that's exactly what my first deal bought and sold for). I'll assume a cash flow of +$140/month, +$180/month, and +$220/month in each of the three years, respectively. Here's what the progression of deals looks like:

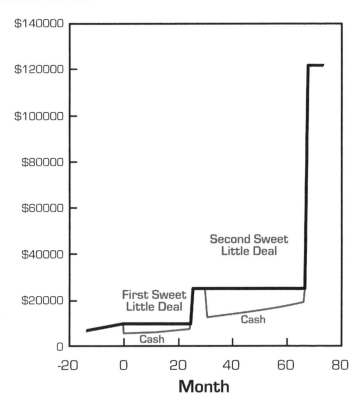

So, if you are in the Small Deals stage, you are already beginning to do well. Here's what you can do to consolidate your good habits and prepare for the next phase: Big Deals.

Actions and Habits to Develop:

1. **Learn about Big Deals by playing Kiyosaki's Cash Flow game.** This amazing teaching tool will give you simulated experience in evaluating big investment and business opportunities.
2. **Educate yourself in the type of Big Deals you want to do.** If you want to buy large rental property, start investigating the market. If you want to invest in businesses, start looking at the business-for-sale section of the paper, talking to people who own businesses in your neighborhood or in a growth area nearby. Take some time to prepare for your first Big Deals and understand the prevailing market conditions, so you can notice when things change and create opportunities.
3. **Learn about Corporations,** especially the tax advantages of corporations. Several of the books in the reading list discuss the benefits of incorporating for businesses and investors with substantial holdings.
4. **Learn about Marketing, Selling and Networking.** As you get into the Big Deals, especially the ones involving businesses, you will need to know how to promote products and create buzz for the things you are doing. This is a fascinating area, and extremely rewarding when you start winning at it. Several of the books recommended at the end of this book address Marketing, Selling and Networking.
5. **Keep your expenses low.**
6. **Continue to avoid consumer debt.**
7. **Continue to Pay Yourself First 10 percent.**
8. **Get on-line.** If you haven't already, learn how to use email and how to surf the web.

Stage Four—Big Deals and Corporations / Brokering Deals

In this stage, we have successfully made some Small Deals, and are now ready to begin making Big Deals. It is typical to begin contemplating Big Deals when your Survival Time is around 1 year. You have learned how to save your own money, use it to make more money, and possibly leveraged other people's money in your Small Deals. So, what makes a deal Big?

Well, the amount of money necessary to get into it is certainly a factor. But another important aspect of a Big Deal is other people's involvement. For example, a 3 bedroom 2 bath house, for which you act as landlord, is probably a Small Deal. But a 20-unit apartment complex, with an on-site manager, grounds maintenance, etc. is a larger scale investment, and requires commitment of other people to make it work.

These two aspects of Big Deals (financial size and number of people involved) usually make it worthwhile to use a corporation to represent the business. For example, it is common in the movie industry to create a new production company (a corporation) to make a movie. This structure allows investors' ownership and participation to be clearly delineated, limits their liability in the event of loss or lawsuit, allows certain important tax advantages, and generally provides a more professional structure for the many participants who are involved.

Corporations

Creation of a corporation can be done inexpensively, and there are self-help books that can show you how to do it (www.nolo. com). My personal experience with creating my first corporation was that I used a legal counsel experienced in filing the articles of incorporation with the state, and experienced in drafting the investor agreements, so that there would be much less chance of dispute later.   The general belief is that good advice in these matters is worth every penny, and can save you literally millions of dollars later. I used a lawyer that was recommended by the lead investor in my company.

One of the most important properties of corporations is the different tax treatment that they are given, compared to individuals. Individuals are taxed largely on their income, and then get to spend what is left. Corporations spend money on their legitimate expenses, and then are taxed on what is left. This important difference is shown on the next pages.

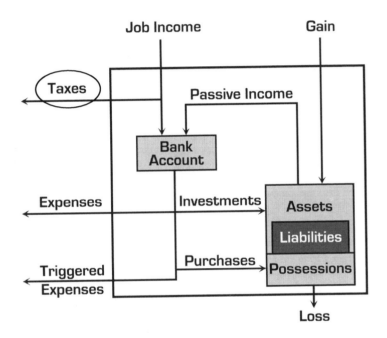

The Flow of Money for Individuals
Taxes are computed *before* expenses are taken out

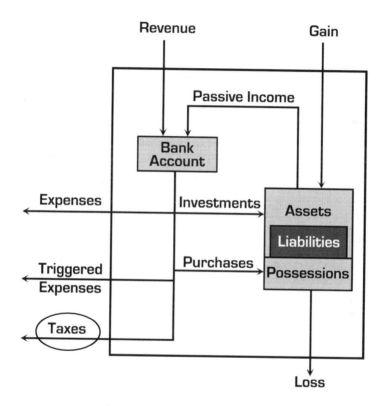

The Flow of Money for Corporations
Taxes are computed *after* expenses are taken out

This means that legitimate expenses for the company (from which you can benefit from indirectly and indirectly) can be paid with pre-tax dollars. Examples of those expenses can include car lease payments, car insurance, car maintenance, business trips, certain meals, etc. It is important to beware, however, that the IRS only permits legitimate business expenses to be deducted.

There are many other aspects of corporations that make them beneficial as the legal structure for your businesses, including limited liability for its investors and directors.

Another advantage in incorporating is the increased legitimacy for your business as compared to a sole proprietorship, for example. It is just much easier for investors to put money into your business when the corporate structure will allow a clear statement of what is given in return for their investment.

Similarly, to create a technology company and attract talented employees, you may need to offer Incentive Stock Options. This will obviously require a corporation.

Disadvantages of incorporation include various fees which must be paid, and increased reporting requirements. For Big enough Deals, these considerations are minor, and more than compensated for by the advantages.

Marketing, Selling and Networking

Another factor which begins to become important as you enter the Big Deals stage is your ability to market and sell. This can take different forms, from selling investors on your ideas, to selling potential customers on your products, to advertising properties for rent, to getting a buzz out about your business. It's possible that you may have gotten all the way through the

Small Deals stage without really having to deal very much with other people. But Big Deals will require you to get people excited about you, your company, and your ideas. These are the skills of marketing and selling.

A related subject is Networking. This is establishing a collection of supportive people who can help you and promote you and your company. I have been extremely fortunate to receive spontaneous help from people who have seen that I am attempting to make a difference for them. There is an incredible power in having other people take up your cause and get their friends excited about it.

Many books have been written about these skills, and I have included my favorite ones in the Recommended Reading section at the end of this book.

Sources of Wealth

There are a great many ways to create or accumulate wealth. Part of the fun of it is in understanding what the different ways are, and choosing a way that suits your personal character and life circumstances. Here is a list of the legitimate methods that actually work for creating and/or accumulating wealth, in approximate order of effort:

1. **Inheritance.** Well, this is an easy one, if you happen to have it in your life circumstances. Someone just leaves you the money or some assets. Gaining wealth this way doesn't require any skill or talent, but *hanging on to it* may.

   Here's the catch, though. Life expectancies are getting longer and longer as medical technologies improve. When I was growing up, in the 1960s, life expectancies were shorter than they are now. My maternal grandparents passed away in their 60s, leaving significant property to my mother and my aunt, who were in their 30s. This gave their financial strength a huge boost, exactly when they were mature enough to use it, setting them both up for a life of prosperity.

   But life expectancies are considerably longer now. It appears that my parents will live healthy lives well into their 80s or longer, meaning that inheritance is not a possibility for me until I will be in my 60s—too late to make a difference in my life. I have always sensed that inheritance would not be a factor in my financial life and have never raised my expectations for it. This attitude has resulted in greater self-sufficiency and a stronger desire to "make it on my own."

2. **Marriage.** Here's another way to get rich: Marry money. It works when you can find it, but increasingly, wealthy people are onto this one and protect themselves via prenuptial agreements, or by simply not getting married at all. Also, it should be pointed out that during the marriage,

the wealth is shared with your spouse; the wealth only becomes independently yours via divorce or inheritance. I know several people for whom this method has proven successful.

3. **Gambling.** This includes lottery and casino winnings, etc., and also could include stock market wins, depending on how you go about it. Needless to say, I don't recommend counting on this one—gambling is playing a game in which the odds are against you, and the most likely outcome is that you lose. I don't actually know anyone who has become wealthy this way.

4. **Conservative Investing.** This can include Certificates of Deposits, Bonds, Treasury Bills, etc. This is a slow, low-risk, low-effort way to grow your money and if you are going to do this, you will need to start early in your life, and/or keep your expenses very low. Read *Your Money or Your Life* by Joe Dominguez and Vicki Robin for a good description of how to succeed with this approach.

5. **Stock Market Investing.** I hear that this works well for some people (but has not worked well for me), provided that you understand the market, technologies, trends, competitors, etc. If you are serious about becoming a stock market investor, I highly recommend *Beating the Street* by Peter Lynch, and *The Intelligent Investor* by Benjamin Graham.

6. **Incentive Stock Options at your Employer.** In Silicon Valley, this is the premier method of becoming wealthy without assuming the risks of business creation, and I know several people who became multi-millionaires at technology companies during the stock market boom of the 1990s. However, by 2008, the stock-options back-dating scandal has had a material effect on several of these companies.

I also know many people who have taken jobs at hot little companies and worked there for years while the company struggles and never executes an exit strategy that leads to the employees realizing any wealth. I also know some people who work for one year at a company, vesting ¼ of their stock options, and then move on, thus building up a diverse portfolio of incentive stock options in technology companies. This approach requires that you have highly marketable skills in today's technology arena. I have personally had a small success with this method, when a company that I worked for was acquired by a larger company.

7. **Real Estate.** This is a classic and powerful method for accumulating wealth, but it requires that you adopt a new persona: the persona of *landlord*. This means finding tenants, dealing with maintenance issues (including sinks and toilets), evicting tenants, living with lost rents, etc. This is definitely not low-effort, but the gains can be spectacular if you have the temperament for it. I don't consider myself a serious real estate investor, but I have personally had a small success with this method, renting and selling a 3 bedroom 2 bath house. If you are serious about becoming a real estate investor, I highly recommend John T. Reed's no-nonsense series of books, beginning with his *How to Get Started in Real Estate Investment.*

8. **Business Ownership.** Another way to accumulate wealth is to own businesses. These businesses can be purchased, but generally require enough up-front capital that they qualify as Big Deals. One of the important distinctions is that, if you work at the business, you have bought yourself a job, not a business. Successful entrepreneurs arrange their businesses so that the businesses can operate without them—this is one of the criteria that makes it possible to sell your business and ultimately realize a profit from it. See *The E-Myth* by Michael Gerber for a thorough discussion of the attitudes of successful business people.

9. **Business Creation.** Rather than purchasing a business, you may have the resources to create a business. This is where

you use your intelligence and life assets, in addition to your financial assets and those assets of other people, to exploit a market opportunity. This falls into the category of entrepreneurship, which can be done on small and large scales alike. Peter Drucker, in *Innovation and Entrepreneurship*, has some very interesting comments on the characteristics of successful entrepreneurs. In particular, he counters the myth that an entrepreneur is necessarily an inventor. Much more often, he contends, the entrepreneur is a synthesizer of existing ideas so as to serve an emerging or existing market, sometimes pulling together ideas that have existed for years but never have been applied together to solve a problem for a particular class of customer. I know several people who have become wealthy this way, and this is the method that I have used with great success in creating my first company, Audience, Inc. (www.audience.com).

10. **Intellectual Property Creation.** This is another powerful way to create wealth—by writing books, recording music, creating films and videos, creating art which can be reproduced, etc. Most of these methods require substantial talent or ability in the particular field of endeavor, as well as suitable skills or counsel in protecting and commercially exploiting the intellectual assets. I know one professor who does not need to worry about tenure at his university because he self-funds his work via his publications for lay readers. This gives him a kind of financial independence, and makes him a much more interesting person as well. Part of the key to this method seems to be "thinking like a producer" as well as "thinking like an artist". If you focus exclusively on creating the art, you may miss the necessary business steps of successfully marketing and distributing your work.

Part IV

Realizing
Your Dreams

Realizing Your Dreams

So far, we have focused heavily on understanding how money works, and the approach to achieving financial independence. But of course, there is much more to life than just financial success. Other important aspects of a person's life can include their relationships, health, spirituality, artistic endeavors, community service, contribution to the world, etc. Ultimately, we may ask what kind of a legacy have we left behind.

The Long-Term Perspective

Most significant achievements are the result of effort sustained over a long period of time. For example, it takes years of study and practice to become proficient at playing a musical instrument. Similarly, building and maintaining a healthy body also takes sustained effort, in the form of exercise, proper nutrition and rest. The only way we can sustain this kind of effort is to have some kind of long-term perspective on what we are trying to accomplish. Sometimes, this might be phrased as a long-term goal (building my piano-playing skill to the point where I can give a concert at the professional level), or it might be expressed as an ongoing activity that serves a long-term purpose (jog, lift weights and stretch, three times a week, to maintain a youthful physique and general strength and health).

In any case, the ability to maintain a long-term perspective and use it to inform our daily actions is the key to building a full and prosperous life.

Here is the tried and tested formula for achieving long-term goals, which I attribute both to Raymond Hull in *How to Get What You Want*, and Anthony Robbins in *Awaken the Giant Within* and *Unlimited Power*:

1. Retreat and decide what you want to accomplish. Write it down and commit to it.
2. Figure out what actions will produce the desired result. Modelling after someone who has already achieved the result is almost always the quickest way to figure out what will work, and results in the shortest path to the goal.
3. Take consistent action to achieve the goal.
4. Regularly revisit the plan to make sure it is working— change course if necessary.

Sustained yet Intermittent Effort

Let's take a closer look at the effort that is required to achieve a long-term goal. For example, working on your health may include jogging three times a week, or lifting weights and stretching three times a week. That effort must be sustained (you have to do it for at least a month to see the benefits, and will want to make it a long-term habit), yet is intermittent (you jog for maybe 45 minutes one day, but then don't jog the next day). These sustained yet intermittent activities seem to be very hard for us to initiate and maintain in our lives. Why is that?

I believe the reason is that we are creatures of habit, and we have natural cycles for our habits. The most natural cycle for habits is *once per day*, and, of course, *once per week* and *once per month* can be natural cycles also. Think for a moment about the habits you have on these natural cycles:

CYCLE TIME	ACTIVITIES
Daily	Sleeping, eating, bathing
Weekly	Work meetings, weekends, parties
Monthly	Paying Bills
Annual	Holidays, vacations, birthdays

It is easiest to build habits that fall naturally onto these cycles. It is hardest to build habits that have different cycles than these, or have no cycle at all. For example, exercise routines often have an *every-other-day* cycle, as necessary to get optimal rest between workouts. Similarly, motor skill and some intellectual skill development also seem to have *every-other-day* cycles, presumably to get optimal transfer of new skills into memory, without burnout. Other activites have no cycle at all, but are *on-demand*, for example, remembering to watch for real estate deals, or maintaining contact with people in your network. It wouldn't make sense to call or write each of your friends every single day, or exactly once a month or exactly once a week, but we need to remember to think of them occasionally and act on it, when there is no natural cycle to remind us.

Building Empowering Habits

How do you build a habit you do every other day, or every third day, or once a week? How do you build a habit of looking for opportunities that appear only occasionally? How do you build a habit of taking occasional spontaneous action?

Here's how: You need to have a way to remind yourself of your desire to do those things, especially while you are trying to build the habit. Once the habit is built, your mind and body will remind you that you haven't exercised in the last few days, or you haven't learned anything new lately, or you haven't done something surprising and nice for your significant other lately.

But until the empowering habit is formed, it is vital to have a reminder of your longer-term goals.

Staying Focused

In modern life, there are many demands on our time. We have calendars and day planners and Palm Pilots to keep track of appointments we make. We have To-Do lists to remind of us of things we need to do, but usually those to-do lists are for work, or for crises (we're moving, so we have a lot of tasks to do in support of that crisis). But where do we keep our long-term goals? And how do we organize our short-term tasks in support of our long-term goals?

I believe the best way to stay focused on these long-term goals is to write them down (Step 1 above) and then keep them in front of you, in your calendar or day planner. What good is a New Year's Resolution or a list of goals if it's on a piece of paper in a drawer? No wonder we forget our resolutions! I write my long-term goals down and keep them in front of me at all times. Every time I open my calendar to make an appointment, I am reminded of my long-term goals.

Here's what my organizer looks like:

 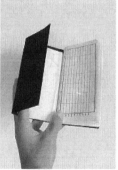 

The organizer is a regular chequebook size, but the front cover has an extra flap that folds up to reveal a place to write my **long-term goals**. The main part of the organizer has pages that come in pairs. The bottom page is a weekly calendar for keeping **appointments**, and the middle page is a place to write **tasks** for the week in support of my long-term goals. I have no trouble remembering what I'm trying to accomplish, because my long-term goals are in front of me whenever I open my organizer to make an appointment. Whenever I have a cancelled appointment, I flip up the top page and look to see how I can use my found time in support of some bigger goal. About once a week, usually on a Sunday evening or Monday morning, I'll revisit my long-term goals, modify them if necessary, and make a note about short-term tasks I want to remember to do this week to make sure I make progress toward my long-term goals.

On the next page is an example of what I might see on a typical week when I flip up the long-term goal flap on my organizer.

Roles and Long-Term Goals

Father	Work	Artist	Friends/Family
Plan trip with girls Michelle birthday	Planning cycle promote project external collaborator	10 original paintings by June	Plan Mom visit Al Celebration
House	**Musician**	**Investor**	
	30-Song Repertoire for coffee-house gigs	on-line banking Buy Assets	
Commun. Serv.	**Health**	**Assets**	
	195 lb. Muscle by August	150 MSFT 300 CSCO	

Roles and Tasks This Week

Father	Work	Artist	Friends/Family
Gifts for Michelle birthday	Prepare Seminar 2nd Pass Plan Speed up Display	study for next painting	Call Larry + Scott
House	**Musician**	**Investor**	
	learn blues tune Setup Cakewalk stereo mic	Set up online banking Pay Bills Call CPA re taxes	
Commun. Serv.	**Health**		
visit Redwood City community center	visit Decathlon Club Buy protein powder		

	SUN 11-Jan	MON 12-Jan	TUE 13-Jan	WED 14-Jan	THU 15-Jan	FRI 16-Jan	SAT 17-Jan
8am							
9am							
10am							
11am		11am mtg				Spike	
noon				Sigcomp		display	
1pm				lunch			
2pm							
3pm			Natcomp				
4pm						Forum	
5pm			Seminar				
6pm							
7pm							
8pm							
9pm							

The Flow of Time and Money Organizer

Let's take a look at the long-term goal under the heading "Health". In my case, I felt I was too thin at 175 lbs. and wanted to put on some muscle. I set my goal of gaining 20 lbs. of muscle by August, which I felt would be achievable with an exercise program and diet I had read about in a bodybuilding magazine. In order to achieve this long-term goal, I was going to need access to some weightlifting equipment and some dietary protein supplements. So, in the Weekly Tasks for that week, I had decided to visit the Decathlon Club and buy a protein powder dietary supplement. Notice that I didn't actually attempt to schedule when I would execute those tasks, I just kept them in front of me so I would be able to do them at the time that worked best with my other activities.

The beauty of the flip-up panel for the long-term goals is that they stay in front of you while the weeks go by. You get a sense of constancy of purpose with your well-considered goals in front of you, always there to remind you what you are trying to accomplish for the long term, and to help you stay focused.

The Process of Mastery

I have been influenced by George Leonard, a sixth degree black belt in Aikido. He describes the process of mastery using the following simple illustration:

That is, the process of learning a new skill has periods of progress, each of which is followed by a slight decline to a plateau at a new higher level. Leonard suggests that the pattern of progress and plateaus is the result of the brain-body mechanism used to assimilate new skills and knowledge.

In the early stages of learning a new skill, such as a tennis backhand stroke, we require conscious effort and concentration on the task. As we repeat the task, it becomes automatic—that is, performance of the task becomes controlled by a subconscious process, which is effectively trained by the conscious mind. Once the subconscious process can perform the task, the conscious mind can be free to build on the new skill, and start working on adding a new one.

In Leonard's diagrams, the plateaus correspond to the practice period in which the new skill is being converted from conscious to subconscious, and the sudden spurts of progress are what we feel when we suddenly notice that we have consolidated a new skill and no longer have to think about it.

But notice the paradox: the learning is happening during the plateaus, precisely when we feel we are making the least progress. This is why the masters recommend diligent and patient study and practice, and don't get worried when the inevitable plateaus happen. To stay on the path, says Leonard, all we have to do is keep learning and practicing. We will be rewarded by the next burst of progress soon enough.

I believe it is possible to make some further observations on this process. Sleep (especially rapid-eye-movement sleep) is known to be an important part of the process of consolidating memory. This is consistent with the observation that learning new skills, especially motor skills, can't really be rushed. They just take many practice sessions, spaced out over many days, and trying to rush them doesn't help. I suspect that cycles of practice and sleep are the key to optimal learning.

Taken together, these observations imply that learning a new skill requires sustained yet intermittent effort (cycles of effort and rest) over a long period while conscious skills are absorbed into subconscious processes. If we show the rest/sleep between the practice sessions, the path of mastery really looks more like this:

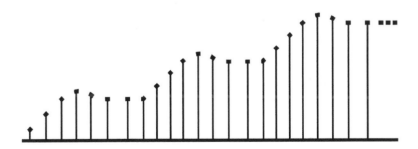

This shows the difficulty of staying on the path even more clearly. Not only do we have periods of no apparent progress (plateaus), but we have breaks between practice sessions, in which we may forget to schedule the next practice session. It takes commitment and discipline to keep coming back to practice under these circumstances.

Here's the good news. If you can get on the path of mastery in a particular area, you can only spend so much time at it. You have to rest between sessions. But in the rest between sessions of one activity, you can be practising another activity, on its own path to mastery. Who says you can only be on one path of mastery? Here's what it looks like with another activity started on its own path:

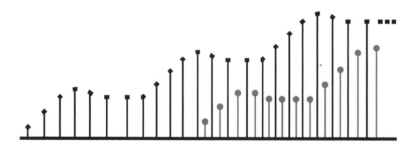

Now, in the rests between practice sessions of one activity, you can be working on a different activity, each on their own paths of mastery. My life is a kind of experiment in pursuing mastery in as many domains as I can. I have always been inspired by Leonardo da Vinci, who was a master of drawing, painting, music, engineering, science, medicine. Was there something special about him that made his feats unattainable by the rest of us, or was it just that he was very efficient about learning and stayed on more paths of mastery than we do?

I personally find that if I spend an hour or two, every two or three days on a skill, I make excellent progress. Any less time than that, and I get rusty. Any more time spent than that, for some activities, seems to result in diminishing returns, and sometimes a feeling of burning out on the activity. Every person will be different, so I recommend that you become sensitive to the "right" amount of time for you to spend on any given task, to maximize your progress over the long run. If you have time left over (you certainly will), consider starting up another Mastery path.

Note that I am not recommending "Jack of all trades, master of none." Just because you are engaged in multiple activities does not mean that you must therefore be dabbling in them. Each one is pursued with single-minded zeal while participating in it. But when resting, you are completely removed from it, and fully free to develop other skills.

The greatest power comes when there begins to be a synergy between the various skills. The more skills you have, the more you find connections between the skills and disciplines. For example, my study of painting has informed my web page designs and photography. My web page designs have allowed me to promote my science work. My science work has caused me to learn how to write computer programs, which create movies and sounds, which extend my studies of art and music. While I do not consider myself a master in any domain yet, I consider that I have been *on the path* of mastery in art, music, science and engineering for 32 years. I have been on the path of mastery of neuroscience for 18 years. I hope to continue to on these paths for decades more. Perhaps some day I will show signs of actually being a master in those arenas—but until then, I will be content to simply be on the path.

Sometimes, after a long time spent on a path, we realize that we have reached our potential, or simply no longer want to be on that path. This happened to me a few times in my life: once after six years of studying karate, and another time after ten years of training in the game of squash. In both cases, I had been fully committed to mastery, but realized that I had reached my potential in these areas, and suddenly felt drawn to invest my time elsewhere.

I agree with Buckminster Fuller, who complained that we have become a society of specialists. Multiple mastery paths is my personal solution to this problem, and I commend it to you.

If you actually take my advice and get on the path of mastery, the following two ideas will speed your progress:

Seek a Role Model or Qualified Teacher

I trained for several hours a day for 2 years in the game of squash, and made very little progress. One day, a young asian man knocked on the glass wall of the squash court and offered to show me the proper way to hold the racquet and hit the ball. He became my coach, and within six months raised my game dramatically, from a weak D-ranked player to a mid-level B. His name was Fan Kwok, and he had been on the Singapore Junior National squash team before traveling to Canada to study.   All the hard work in the world on my part could not have substituted for qualified instruction from this talented coach. There's just no substitute for knowing what you're doing. If you are attempting to build basic skills in an arena where there are qualified instructors, engage the services of the best one you can find. Note that this advice applies not just to sports, but to intellectual, artistic, financial pursuits, etc.

Study the Masters

To some people, it might seem obvious that studying the masters is a valuable way to speed your progress down the path of mastery. However, weren't we always punished for copying someone else's work in school? Or told that copying would stifle our creativity? What's the difference? When is copying good, and when is it bad?

One form of copying is plagiarism, that is, passing off someone else's work as your own. Obviously this is dishonest and serves no-one.

However, there is a time when copying is a very valuable exercise. When I say "study the masters", I mean, *as a learning exercise*, duplicate the works of the masters, so as to understand how they put things together, and to build a practical understanding of what works and what doesn't. Cezanne filled more than twenty notebooks with studies of paintings and sculptures from the Louvre. Picasso studied other artists so intensely that he was regarded as without his own style for the first several years of his career. Another tradition in which copying is respected as a valid learning method is Jazz music. Since so little of the art is written down, musicians are expected to listen to recordings of past masters and "transcribe" (that is, copy) their work while learning what works and what doesn't. Jazz pianist/vocalist Diana Krall recommends learning the entire repertoire of three past masters as part of the learning process. Bruce Hornsby was deeply influenced by a bootleg copy of a concert by Leon Russell, and extensively studied the work of jazz great Keith Jarrett. I have done studies of paintings by Picasso, Cezanne, Kandinski, Bruni, Sabzi, and studied the instrumental and vocal recordings of Elton John, Bruce Hornsby, Robben Ford and James Taylor. And in my science work, I have benefited tremendously by duplicating the work that is considered state of the art, before going on to attempt to improve upon it. In the early stages of development, copying is an incredibly powerful way of accelerating the learning process. After copying successfully for a while, you will be ready to discard copying, as you develop your own unique style.

I believe that some teachers, in a well-meaning attempt to foster creativity and discourage cheating, have failed to make the important distinction between plagiarism and studying the masters, and in so doing, have cut off their students from a powerful learning tool that has served many developing masters well. If this happened to you, you might benefit by revisiting your training methods and incorporating this one into your approach.

Part V

Contributing
To The World

Contributing to the World

So, what is the point of having great wealth, education, relation-ships, health and organization? Just to say you did it? To prove you could win a difficult game? I assume that I can do that, and in fact, I assume we can all do that, if we choose to. I need a bigger reason. The only reason that makes sense to me is to make a contribution to society, a difference to the many people, one at a time. This is my reason for writing this book.

In 1998, I was working as a researcher, trying to understand how the brain works and build new types of computers that work like the brain. For the first time in my career, I had cre-ated the possibility of working on a project that I felt could change the world, and was personally interesting to me as well. But I could see that my project was going to take a long time to make a difference to the world, at least 4 years, maybe 10 years (and it did take 10 years, until 2008, before it was selling a commercially successful product). And I began to ask, "What could I do **now** to make the biggest possible contribution to the world?"

Well, that question was too general. The world, as a whole, is too big for me to reasonably contemplate affecting. So, instead, I asked, "What is the biggest problem in people's daily lives that I can meaningfully address?" I figured that if I could help a lot of people individually, that would have a chance of making a difference to the world as a whole. My answer was: Most people's daily lives are spent in worry about not having enough money, and not having enough time, watching their lives slip away while their dreams fade from them, while they work at some unfulfilling job to get paid less than they feel they are worth. And most of the problems could be solved, if only they understood better how to work with time and money.

I decided in that moment that I would spend a part of my time, and a part of my money, trying to teach people how time and money work, and trying to help them solve these kinds of problems.

Try asking yourself this question:

"What is the biggest problem in people's daily lives that I can meaningfully address?"

Your answer will be different from mine. Help even one person solve a problem, and you make a difference to that person. If you can generalize your solution method and share it with a lot of people, you will make a contribution to the world.

Higher Purpose

I have always felt a sense of destiny or higher purpose in my life, although I have no way of explaining where it may come from. Perhaps it is simply something I want to believe and I am creating a self-fulfilling prophecy. Or perhaps there are just some things we are better suited to do, based on our upbringing, inherited traits, etc., and we feel rewarded when we stumble upon them. Or perhaps there is a deeper structure to the universe and in our rare moments of silence we can hear its pure whisper.

Wherever our Higher Purpose comes from, I sense its presence and I feel that a mention of it has a place in this book. My first observation is that your Higher Purpose is a quiet call that, at first, is drowned out by the loud noises of daily life. We have these pressing demands on our time, many of which are caused by our need to make a living, and if we only listen to these loud, insistent noises, we will never hear the quiet urging that is our Higher Purpose.

Everyone will have a different way of accessing the silence in which a sense of Higher Purpose can be perceived. For some people it is in prayer or meditation, for others it is in the flow state of a sport, or in the feeling of a brush on canvas, or in a wilderness retreat. The point is to be sensitive to where you are when your Higher Purpose calls to you, and create regular opportunities to visit it and get to know it, at a deeper and deeper level each time. After a while, the quiet whisper becomes a powerful presence that shows itself increasingly in daily life.

Courage and Truth to Self

My second observation about Higher Purpose and contribution to the world has to do with the courage required to follow it. When we get an inkling of some larger scheme for the world, and the feeling that perhaps we have a role to play in it, we will naturally question it. We have been raised to be modest, to fit in. Who am I to think such big thoughts? Can I risk drawing attention to myself before I am sure that my ideas will be accepted?

It takes great courage to manifest your full potential. That is the grand challenge for all of us. It does not serve you or the world to hide your capabilities and talents, or to minimize your contribution because it might make other people feel insecure. On the contrary, expressing your full potential shows others that it is safe to truly be yourself, and inspires others to do the same for themselves.

Following a sense of Higher Purpose usually means some kind of renunciation of what you were doing previously. In my career, I had prepared diligently to do interesting research, but for some reason, after getting my doctorate, I lost my confidence, and instead of taking a leadership position, I joined two consecutive companies that asked me to do work for which I was not really suited. It look me about five years before I finally realized that I needed to be truthful to myself and to return to the work I was doing at Caltech and start building on that. In that transition period, I joked with some friends, "I'm tired of working on other people's dumb ideas—I want to work on *my own* dumb ideas!"

The reason that such a transition takes so much courage is because it makes a public statement that you are going to change directions, with no guarantee that you will succeed in the new direction. By definition, pursuit of this kind of success requires that you risk public failure. And in most cases, you will lose support that you enjoyed previously. Every entrepreneur who stops working for someone else and starts working for himself (or herself) has to go through this process. And every one I have spoken to (and myself also) will tell you they were terrified as they ventured down the unknown new path. There is just a point at which you make the assessment that the new path is the only one that is right for you, you are prepared to handle whatever the world throws at you, and you go for it. I've had similar moments of courage in a fire-walk (led by Tony Robbins), performing music publicly for the first time, starting my first company, writing this chapter of this book, and launching my hang glider for the first time at 2500 feet.

Have the courage to be truthful to yourself. Retreat regularly from the noises of daily life so that you can sense your Higher Purpose. And have the courage to make a difference to the world.

The Mentor System

There is a quiet and powerful tradition that is rarely talked about. I have been extremely fortunate to receive of this tradition, which I will call the Mentor System. It is the tradition of passing down knowledge to the next generation, but not just in a simple or personally removed way—my experience of this has been that it is a deeply moving and generous way, something very closely related to a sense of Higher Purpose.

I have been fortunate to receive twice in this tradition. In 1984, I was introduced by Physics professor David Atherton to a businessman named Allan Crawford. Al had asked Prof.

Atherton if there were any students in the fourth year Engineering Physics class that were showing particular promise. I had spent my entire spring break in the basement of the physics building, building my thesis project (when only a written report was required), and had just recently gotten it working—a signal processor that could change the pitch of musical sounds in real-time. Al met with me, liked what I had accomplished, gave me a business card, and told me to look him up if I ever visited the Vancouver area.

Well, I did take a job in the Vancouver area, and so I began keeping in touch with Al, building a new version of the pitch-shifter at his offices in Vancouver, and meeting people he thought I should get to know. After three years of working and learning at the job I had taken, Al told me he thought I should go back to school and get a Ph.D., and if I did, he would help to sponsor me. He knew of a scholarship intended for working engineers to go back to graduate school, in which the government would provide matching funding if a company would provide equal funding. Al offered to be the industrial sponsor and made arrangements with his contacts in the government to make the scholarship happen. Over a five year period from 1987-1992, Al contributed $75,000 to my education, with no strings attached, just the hope that when I was ready to start a company, we would work together. And in the meantime, he has been introducing me to influential people and teaching me about business in countless ways.

Now here's the amazing thing. I'm not the only person that Al has done this for. In May 2000, a group of us organized a Forum to honor Al for his contributions to our careers. Al has made this kind of generous contribution to literally dozens of young engineers, scientists, businesspeople, and technologists over the last forty years. It is a part of how he has created a strong and loyal organization, but I know that for him it is much more than that. He sees himself as a catalyst for us, and he is passing on a tradition that was passed down to him by his mentor, Dr. M. MacDonnell, whom he regards as the fundamental catalyst for his own career.

I also consider that I have received of the mentoring tradition by my Ph.D. advisor at Caltech, Professor Carver Mead. He created a phenomenal environment for his students, and has generously shared his knowledge with several generations of students for over forty years. At the end of my three-year tour of duty at Caltech, I spent a day with him, driving around the Los Gatos mountains and talking about life, business, and predicting the future of technology. At the end of that conversation, I wanted to thank him for teaching me so much, and wondered aloud how one could ever repay such a debt. He said to me, "Lloyd, that's not the kind of debt you pay back. That's the kind of debt you pay forward."

I sense that I am heading into the period of my life where I make good on my desire to pay these debts forward, just as Carver and Al have paid them forward to me. Time will tell if I am able to serve successfully as a mentor.

It may be tempting to think that my experience of having been mentored by these great leaders must be a rare exception, and that such a thing would only happen to a lucky few. I suggest that you turn the situation around and look at it from the point of view of the Mentor. Here you have a person who has succeeded in life, and is ready to begin the process of paying forward what he (or she) has received from past mentors. Actually, the hard thing from the Mentor's point of view is finding young people who are hard-working and open-minded enough that they are worth investing this kind of time into. I think those are two of the qualities that have made it easy for people to choose me as a protégé—not necessarily intelligent, just hard-working and open-minded. It's amazing how hard work and open-mindedness, accumulated over time with steadiness of purpose, can result in the appearance of intelligence. There are more mentors out there than you might think, but they are very choosy about how they spend their time.

In *Rich Dad, Poor Dad*, Robert Kiyosaki tells the story of the wealthy friends who talk about young people who only ever ask them for either a loan or a job; no-one ever asks them how they got wealthy. Mentors aren't interested in giving away money, because they know that's futile. They are interested in teaching life principles to open-minded students who will work hard to apply those principles, and carry on their tradition by passing those principles on.

Legacy

Ultimately, how do you want to be remembered? Many people don't start thinking about this until it is too late to create the legacy they would like. I believe that we don't have to wait until retirement to think about legacy. In fact, we are creating our legacy throughout our lives, whether we realize it or not, and I believe that we create a more enjoyable and exciting life if we look at it this way as we go along.

This entire book has been, indirectly, about creating a legacy. How you spend your money and how you spend your time determines your fate, and ultimately determines how you will be remembered. Invest heavily in yourself so you will have strength and wisdom to share with others, and leave a legacy of people who have been influenced by your time here on Earth.

May you live life to the fullest!

Recommended Reading

George S. Clason, *The Richest Man in Babylon*, Bantam Books, 1955.

Stephen R. Covey, *The Seven Habits of Highly Effective People: Powerful Lessons in Personal Change*, Simon and Schuster, 1989.

Joe Dominguez and Vicki Robin, *Your Money or Your Life: Transforming Your Relationship with Money and Achieving Financial Independence*, Penguin Group Press, 1992.

Peter Drucker, *Innovation and Entrepreneurship*.

Betty Edwards, *Drawing on the Right Side of the Brain*, Tarcher/ Putnam, 1989.

Buckminster Fuller, *Education Automation*, 1962, and *Approaching the Benign Environment*.

Michael J. Gelb, *How to Think like Leonardo da Vinci*, Delacorte Press, 1998.

Raymond Hull, *How to Get What You Want*, Hawthorn Books, 1969.

Robert T. Kiyosaki and Sharon L. Lechter, *Rich Dad, Poor Dad: What the Rich Teach Their Kids About Money - That the Poor and Middle Class Do Not!*, TechPress Inc.,1997.

George Leonard, "Playing for Keeps: The art of mastery in sport and life", *Esquire Magazine*, 1987.

Peter Lynch, *Beating the Street*, Fireside Books, 1994.

Steven Pinker, *How the Mind Works*, W.W.Norton, 1997.

John T. Reed, *How to Get Started in Real Estate Investment: Practical, ethical, real-world advice for beginning investors,* www.johntreed.com, 2000.

Anthony Robbins, *Awaken the Giant Within,* Summit Books, 1991.

Thomas J. Stanley, William D. Danko, *The Millionaire Next Door: The Surprising Secrets of America's Wealthy,* Pocket Books, 1996.

Robert Wright, *The Moral Animal,* Vintage Books, 1994.

Index

Photograph Credit: Laura Brisbee

About the Author

LLOYD WATTS has invested successfully in real estate, stocks, and intellectual property licensing. He is the author of five patents, and holds a Ph.D. from the California Institute of Technology. He is the founder, Chairman, and Chief Technology Officer of Audience, Inc. He is an accomplished painter, musician, hang glider pilot and photographer.

www.lloydwatts.com

The Flow of Time and Money

Book: Additional copies of "The Flow of Time and Money" may be ordered at the price of $15.99/copy, plus shipping and handling charges. Please use the contact information below to place an order.

The Flow of Time and Money
Megawatt Media Corporation
1931 Old Middlefield Way, Suite 221
Mountain View, CA 94043

www.flowoftimeandmoney.com